NEUROPLASTICITY

Exercises to Improve Cognitive Flexibility,
Conquer Trauma & PTSD, Change Bad Habits,
Eliminate Depression and So Much More!

ADRIAN WINSHIP

© **Copyright 2019 - All rights reserved.**

The content contained within this book may not be reproduced, duplicated or transmitted without direct written permission from the author or the publisher.

Under no circumstances will any blame or legal responsibility be held against the publisher, or author, for any damages, reparation, or monetary loss due to the information contained within this book. Either directly or indirectly.

Legal Notice:
This book is copyright protected. This book is only for personal use. You cannot amend, distribute, sell, use, quote or paraphrase any part, or the content within this book, without the consent of the author or publisher.

Disclaimer Notice:
Please note the information contained within this document is for educational and entertainment purposes only. All effort has been executed to present accurate, up to date, and reliable, complete information. No warranties of any kind are declared or implied. Readers acknowledge that the author is not engaging in the rendering of legal, financial, medical or professional advice. The content within this book has been derived from various sources. Please consult a licensed professional before attempting any techniques outlined in this book.

By reading this document, the reader agrees that under no circumstances is the author responsible for any losses, direct or indirect, which are incurred as a result of the use of information contained within this document, including, but not limited to, — errors, omissions, or inaccuracies.

Table of Contents

Preface ix

Introduction xiii

What Is Neuroplasticity? xiii

PART 1: INTRODUCTION AND EVIDENCE OF NEUROPLASTICITY 1

Chapter 1: What Can You Expect From This Book? 3

    Why is this book good for you? 4

    What can you do after reading this book? 5

    Why should you read this book now? 5

    What are you thinking? 6

    What do you fear? 6

    What are you struggling with? 7

    What are your biggest day-to-day frustrations? 8

    What challenges are you currently facing? 9

    What are the main benefits you'll get from this book? 9

    How can you apply the concepts in this book to your life practically? 12

    What problem(s) will you be able to overcome? 13

Chapter 2: What Is Neuroplasticity? 14

    Definition of Neuroplasticity 15

    Two Types of Brain Cells 16

    Case Studies That Provide Evidence of Neuroplasticity 27

    Can We Influence the Process of Neuroplasticity? 32

    All About Neuroplasticity Games 35

Chapter 3: How Age Is Related to Neuroplasticity 38

    What Does Science Have to Say? 40

Chapter 4: What Is Neurogenesis? 43

    Neurogenesis vs. Neuroplasticity 45

    Where Does Neurogenesis Occur? 47

    How Neurogenesis and Neuroplasticity Work Together 48

    How to Increase Neurogenesis 50

Chapter 5: Why Your Environment Matters 54

    What Is Environmental Enrichment? 56

    A Study About Environmental Enrichment and Stress-Related Systems 59

    Other Studies 60

    Environmental Enrichment Is Truly Important 63

PART 2: EXERCISES FOR COGNITIVE FLEXIBILITY 65

Chapter 6: What Is Cognitive Flexibility? 67

Aspects of Cognitive Flexibility 69

Chapter 7: Exercises to Improve Cognitive Flexibility 71

Before Beginning These Exercises 72

Interpersonal Exercises 76

Exercises of Movement and Sensory Stimulation 82

Mental Exercises 88

Final Thoughts on Exercises to Improve Cognitive Flexibility and Neuroplasticity 93

PART 3: CONQUERING TRAUMA AND PTSD THROUGH NEUROPLASTICITY 95

Chapter 8: Trauma and PTSD Defined 97

What Is Trauma? 98

What Is PTSD? 100

Chapter 9: How Are PTSD and Trauma Related to Neuroplasticity? 103

Specific Regions of the Brain Affected by PTSD 105

Learned Helplessness 107

Chapter 10: Conquering Trauma and PTSD Using Neuroplasticity 111

Overview 112

Creating New Neural Pathways to Conquer Trauma and PTSD 115

PART 4: CHANGING BAD HABITS 127

Chapter 11: The Science of Habit Formation 129

- Myelination 131
- Why Is Starting New Habits Difficult? 134
- Strategies for Forming New Habits and Making Them Stick 139
- Changing Current Habits 141
- Habit Formation and Neuroplasticity 147

PART 5: ELIMINATING DEPRESSION 149

Chapter 12: Brains Suffering From Depression 151

- Normal Brain vs. Depressed Brain 153
- Decreased Neuroplasticity 155
- PET Scans of Depressed Brain 156

Chapter 13: Using the Principle of Repetition to Eliminate Depression 158

- The Trouble with Positive Thinking 159
- The Power of Words 160
- Stimulating Our Brains to Encode Joy 164
- The Power of Reframing 167
- Overcoming Depression Through Neuroplasticity 170

PART 6: DEFEATING PROCRASTINATION AND OTHER ISSUES 173

Chapter 14: What Is Procrastination? 175

- The Psychology of Procrastination 176
- How Neuroplasticity Impacts Procrastination 176

Defeating Procrastination Through Neuroplasticity 178

Chapter 15: The Power of Neuroplasticity 180

Defeating Addiction Through Neuroplasticity 181

Defeating Phobias Through Neuroplasticity 182

Defeating Insomnia Through Neuroplasticity 183

Neuroplasticity and Lifestyle...184

Chapter 16: Binaural Beats and Brainwave Entrainment: Does It Increase Neuroplasticity? 186

What Is Brainwave Entrainment? 187

The Different Brain Waves and Their Proposed Benefits...189

Evidence Showing How Binaural Beats or Brainwave Entrainment Help Neuroplasticity 195

The Benefits of Brainwave Entrainment or Binaural Beats 197

Finding the Best Resources 201

Bibliography..203

Preface

I've often heard people around me say, "I'm depressed." But for most of them, they may just be feeling down or sad. In reality, depression isn't as simple as being sad. It's much more than that. I should know, because I suffer from depression. In my last book, I talked about how I met an amazing woman who changed my life, but then left this world too soon. When she took her life, it broke me. But it also made me stronger.

Although she wasn't able to overcome her depression, I made a promise to her that I would fight to overcome mine. As I've said, she changed my life for the better, and I didn't want to tarnish her memory by giving up. So in an attempt to help myself, I started doing a lot of research. This is where I found a very interesting concept known as neuroplasticity.

This is a concept backed by science that basically states that we all have the power to change our brains or minds in order to change our lives. Personally, when I first read about neuroplasticity, I didn't think much of it. The whole concept seemed too good to be true, so I kept looking for other treatment options for my condition. But as I continued with my research, neuroplasticity kept coming up. Finally I thought to myself, "What will I lose if I learn more about it?"

Instead of wallowing in my depression, I decided to invest my time in learning all about neuroplasticity: what it really is, what the benefits are, what the "scientific evidence" says and more. The more I learned about it, the more I realized how helpful this concept is! And it wasn't just helpful for depression. Neuroplasticity can be applied to other issues as well, such as procrastination (something I am also guilty of), PTSD, trauma, changing bad habits, and so much more.

As I learned the science behind neuroplasticity, I realized why it works. Then I started learning about the different strategies of neuroplasticity. Now, I can confidently say that I am a much better person because of it. No, I haven't totally gotten rid of my depression, but I know that I am on a path towards healing. Neuroplasticity has brought a new kind of positivity and hope into my life, and I am so thankful that I decided to learn more about it.

I have gathered some helpful information to share with others. Simply put, this book is for anyone who wants to take a proactive step toward changing their life for the better. Whether you want to overcome depression, change bad habits or simply understand this concept more, I hope this book can help you as much as my own personal research has helped me.

As I have learned the hard way, there's really no need to stay in a dark place for the rest of your life. As difficult as things may seem now, there's always a way to make a change. Hopefully, this book will help you pick yourself up and start your journey towards healing.

INTRODUCTION

What Is Neuroplasticity?

The human brain is a wonderful thing. It's constantly undergoing changes each time we experience things in our lives. Think about it: How different are your thoughts and behaviors now than they were 20 years ago? Although we don't really think about this change, this is actually neuroplasticity in action. At its very core, neuroplasticity is any change in the organization and structure of the brain as we learn, adapt and have different experiences.

As you repeat thoughts or emotions, you are reinforcing neural pathways. Each time you have a new thought, you start creating a new way of being. As small as these changes are, if you repeat them enough, this leads to a change in how your brain functions. When it comes to neuroplasticity, this is referred to as the "muscle building" aspect of the brain. The more we repeat a certain emotion, action, experience or thought, the stronger it becomes. And when you don't repeat these things, they tend to fade away. As the old adage goes, "Out of sight, out of mind."

Another way to look at neuroplasticity is that it's the physical basis of why repeating actions or thoughts increase their power. As time goes by, these become a part of our being. Literally speaking, we become what we do and think.

Although some people haven't even heard about neuroplasticity, it's actually at work throughout our lives. The connections in our brain are constantly either becoming weaker or stronger, depending on what you are repeating. For younger people, their brains are still easy to change. But as we grow older, change doesn't occur as easily as it did in the past. With age, our brains lose some of their plasticity, which, in turn, causes us to become more "fixed" in terms of how we perceive, learn and think.

Our brains are key to everything we do and think. When you learn how to harness the power of neuroplasticity, you will be able to improve your thoughts and actions. Neurofeedback works with the basic principles of neuroplasticity to help you control your own mind.

In this book, you will learn all about neuroplasticity. Before going into the strategies of applying this to your life, we will first be talking about the science behind neuroplasticity to help you understand the concept better. As we delve into this concept, things will hopefully become clearer for you.

Neuroplasticity is the incredible capacity of the brain to adapt and change. It's the physiological changes that occur in your brain as a result of all the experiences and interactions you have with your environment. Although you have likely already reached adulthood, this doesn't mean that you cannot change your life or the bad habits that you have learned through the years. As mentioned, the brain is constantly changing. As long as you understand and accept this concept, neuroplasticity becomes a lot easier to apply.

With neuroplasticity, you can recondition your brain and reorganize your thoughts to make the changes you want to see in your life. Of course, there are proper ways to do this, which we will be learning later on. With that being said, let's begin by learning more about what you can expect from this book.

As A Token of My Gratitude...

http://bit.ly/BinauralBeatsCollection

I'd like to offer you this amazing resource. Click on the picture above or navigate to the website below the picture to join my exclusive email list. Upon joining, you will receive these incredible binaural beats. The last chapter of this book goes more in-depth to this technology.

I wanted to give you the opportunity to go ahead and start reaping the benefits from this now rather than waiting until you get to the end of this book. I have used them in my own personal healing.

You will simply need to wear headphones and play the audio files to experience the benefits.

PART 1

INTRODUCTION AND EVIDENCE OF NEUROPLASTICITY

"Neurons that fire together, wire together."

- *Donald Hebb, Canadian Neuropsychologist*

Neuroplasticity

CHAPTER 1

What Can You Expect From This Book?

Although the subject of this book may seem unfamiliar and quite intimidating to a lot of people, it's really not. This book is all about neuroplasticity and how you can apply it to your life. Whether you suffer from depression or PTSD, or simply want to break some of your bad habits, this book will be a valuable resource for you. You will learn a mixture of scientific concepts and practical applications.

Through this book, you will learn more about your brain and the incredible power of neuroplasticity, and how you can use it to transform your life. Of course, improving your life doesn't stop with the learning you acquire. No matter how many times you read this book and other resources about neuroplasticity, if you don't have a willingness to make a change, nothing will happen.

As you learn new things from this book, you should also start reflecting on your own life. Think about the things you want to change, and how you can change them through everything you're about to learn. Then you can start sharing your knowledge and promoting the power of your brain to serve as a real-life example of how neuroplasticity actually works!

Why is this book good for you?

We all want to change something in our lives. No matter how happy we are with life, there will always be something we can improve upon. This is even more significant when you suffer from a mental condition such as anxiety, depression or trauma. No matter who you are and where you are right now in the process of change, this book will be beneficial for you. As you go through the different chapters, you will learn more about the power of your brain and how neuroplasticity can improve your life. And when you're armed with the right knowledge, you can start changing your life for the better.

What can you do after reading this book?

The very best thing you can do after you read this book is to become a healthier, more productive person. You'll be able to understand more, and through this new self-love and self-improvement, you can also start to be more caring of others. This book can help you make a huge impact on your life, as well as your relationships with other people. As long as you apply what you learn in this book, good things will surely follow.

Why should you read this book now?

If you've reached this part, it means you're already reading. Good for you! But if you need more convincing, you should keep reading this book, because it can potentially change your life for the better. If you were like me, stuck in a rut, this book will help you help yourself. If you're also like me and you've had an enlightening, life-changing experience that made you decide to pick yourself up from rock bottom, then this book will help you learn things that you never even thought were possible. And even if you're a well-adjusted person who simply wants to improve yourself, this book will help you do just that. So keep reading!

What are you thinking?

Right now, what thought is running through your mind? Are you having anxious thoughts? Positive thoughts? A little bit of both? Those thoughts that run through your mind are causing your brain to grow, change and develop. So you should be careful about the thoughts that you allow yourself to keep thinking over and over again. Later on, you will learn how your thoughts, experiences and actions have the power to change your brain. Creating new connections, strengthening existing connections and losing connections in the brain all happen depending on what you do in your life.

What do you fear?

Fear is something we all have to deal with. But just because you're afraid of something, this doesn't mean that you should cower in your fear and forget to live your life. No matter what kind of experiences you have had in the past, you should find the courage to face your fears head-on until you're able to overcome them. This is another practical application of neuroplasticity. Through this, you can teach yourself to deal with your fears. Although it won't be easy, overcoming your fears is entirely possible. As you learn more, you can come up with your own strategies to help you beat your fears and lead a richer, fuller life.

What are you struggling with?

Struggles are also a part of life. At one point or another, we all struggle with problems within ourselves, with the people around us and with our environments. But instead of looking at struggles as something that might defeat you, think of them as challenges and learning opportunities. Remember that how you think of things has a significant effect on how your brain processes them. When you think negatively, you may find it more difficult to deal with your struggles. But when you think positively, you may find it easier to find solutions to problems and strategies to overcome those struggles.

- **Bad Habits**

Are you struggling with bad habits? Well, you're not the only one. We all have our own bad habits, which may have started when we were younger, and which we have carried as we grew into the adults we are now. Just because you have these bad habits and have been struggling with them doesn't mean that it's too late to change them. As you will learn, neuroplasticity (and other brain-focused exercises) can help you break these bad habits. They can also help you learn new habits that will make you a healthier and better person.

- **Painful Memories**

Do you struggle with painful memories? Personally, this was one of the biggest challenges I had to face in my life. In fact, I am still in the process of overcoming my struggle with painful memories. Even though I haven't totally forgotten these memories, I have started working on them. Neuroplasticity is a powerful thing. You may not be able to totally forget the memories that make you feel broken, but you can help yourself break free of them. In doing this, you can focus on the more positive things in life, and on the things that make you happy.

What are your biggest day-to-day frustrations?

As you go through your daily routine, there may be things that always seem to make you feel frustrated. These may be simple things or big things. Either way, they can make you want to tear your hair out each time you experience them. There's no time like the present to start working on these day-to-day frustrations. As you learn more about neuroplasticity, you should start formulating a plan to deal with those things that make you feel aggravated each day. If you're able to execute the plan you have created, then you won't have to deal with these frustrations. Doesn't that sound better?

What challenges are you currently facing?

Think about the challenges you're currently facing in your life right now. Are you depressed? Do you suffer from PTSD? Do you feel like there is so much negativity in your life that you need to break free of it? If you're facing any kind of challenge right now, neuroplasticity can help you with it. I keep mentioning this because it's what this book is all about! I personally have applied neuroplasticity in my life, and I have seen how much it changed me. Changing your life is a process. Sometimes it's a lifelong process wherein you just keep finding ways to enrich your life and make it better, and one way to do this is by overcoming those challenges that plague you.

What are the main benefits you'll get from this book?

Purchasing and downloading this book is one of the best decisions you could have made for yourself. Neuroplasticity is a relatively new concept that is changing how people think all over the world. Since it was discovered, scientists, researchers and other experts have dedicated countless studies to neuroplasticity because of its incredible potential. From experiments conducted on animals to those conducted on human subjects and patients, we will be discussing some of these studies throughout the book. One thing they have in common is that they provide evidence on how beneficial neuroplasticity is. And since this book is all about that concept, you will be able to get enjoy great benefits too!

- **Enhances cognition and improves intelligence.**

Since neuroplasticity encourages the growth and development of the brain, you can use it to enhance your cognitive functions and improve your intelligence. There are certain exercises that you can do to become smarter. And as you will soon discover, these exercises all promote neuroplasticity. Even if you've graduated from school and you've already learned a lot from your profession, you can still push yourself further. And if you feel like you didn't make the most out of the time you spent in school, you can continue or restart your learning to make your brain stronger and encourage its plasticity.

- **Protects against degenerative diseases such as Alzheimer's and Parkinson's.**

Another great benefit of neuroplasticity is that it can help protect you against degenerative diseases that affect the brain. Studies have shown that those who don't "use" their brains are more susceptible to these kinds of diseases. If you want to maintain the health, strength and structure of your brain, you must keep using it. This means that you should keep on learning new things, having new experiences and interacting with new people. There are many ways you can do this, which, we will be discussing later on in the book. With practice, you can even come up with your own strategies and brain-strengthening exercises that will improve your neuroplasticity!

- **Mitigates impaired cognitive function and aging.**

We all have to undergo the aging process. This is a fact of life that we cannot escape from. But when it comes to our brains, we can use neuroplasticity to lessen the impairment of our cognitive functions that come with aging. This is another huge benefit of this book. Imagine being a 60- or 70-year-old with a mind that's still as sharp as that of a 30- or 40-year-old? Although your body might weaken or succumb to the effects of the aging process, you can alleviate these effects by learning how to apply neuroplasticity to your life.

- **Makes your brain adapt to changes you may come across in life.**

Neuroplasticity also helps your brain adapt to any changes you may have in your life. You may have heard the saying "You can't teach old dogs new tricks." This is the opposite of neuroplasticity, so you must stop believing this saying. It's totally possible for you to adapt to your situation and to any changes, and the easiest way to do this so by using your brain. A powerful brain gives you the ability to adapt to such changes no matter how extreme they may seem. And when you're able to do this, you will notice that life becomes a whole lot easier.

- **Gain new experiences**

Everything you will learn from this book will also help you gain new experiences. As you see the improvements in your life, you will become more courageous in terms of how you approach life and all of its challenges. The more courageous you are, the more you will have the willingness to get out there and experience new things. This, in turn, helps forge new connections in your brain. So it's like a beneficial cycle that will help you move forward each and every day.

How can you apply the concepts in this book to your life practically?

This part depends on you. In this book, you will be learning all about neuroplasticity and how you can apply it in your life. We will define the concept and discuss it from a scientific point of view to help you understand it better.

What Can You Expect From This Book?

Then we will be going into different exercises, tips and strategies that will give you a better idea of how you can apply the concepts to your life. As you will soon discover, applying these concepts in a practical way isn't that difficult. As long as you understand the concepts and why they work, you can apply them to your life easily.

What problem(s) will you be able to overcome?

Neuroplasticity can help you overcome all sorts of problems! From simple things like having too many negative thoughts to trying to break bad habits and solve more complex and overwhelming problems that involve your mind (such as procrastination, depression, trauma and more), you will have the potential to work through these issues using what you learn in the different chapters of this book. With that being said, let's begin your journey into neuroplasticity!

CHAPTER 2

What Is Neuroplasticity?

When it comes to neuroplasticity, there is a lot to learn. It isn't a simple concept that you can read about and understand in a single moment. After learning the definition of neuroplasticity, most people may not really understand all of its implications. But this is an incredible concept that has the potential to change your life for the better.

Before you can learn how to apply neuroplasticity to your life, you must first understand what it is. From the definition of neuroplasticity to the more scientific concepts behind it, we will be covering a lot of topics in this chapter. All of this information will help you understand neuroplasticity more profoundly.

Definition of Neuroplasticity

Neuroplasticity refers to the ability of the brain to reorganize itself. This happens when the brain creates new neural connections throughout your life. Neuroplasticity allows your brain's nerve cells (neurons) to compensate for any disease and injury, as well as to adjust the activities of these cells in response to any changes in your environment, or to any new experiences.

The reorganization of the brain occurs through various mechanisms, such as "axonal sprouting." In this process, axons that are undamaged grow nerve endings in order to reconnect the links of neurons that have been severed or injured. These undamaged axons may also sprout nerve endings in order to connect with other nerve cells that are also undamaged. This process creates new neural pathways that are required to perform a required function.

For instance, if one of your brain's hemispheres gets damaged, the hemisphere that remains intact may start performing some of the damaged hemisphere's functions.

In this way, your brain compensates for the damage by reorganizing itself and creating new connections between the neurons that remain intact. But in order for your neurons to reconnect, you must stimulate them through activity.

Neuroplasticity is also known as brain malleability or brain plasticity. Either way, learning how to make the most out of this process will allow you to make significant changes in how you think and act.

Two Types of Brain Cells

The basic building blocks of living things are known as "cells." Our bodies are composed of trillions of these cells, and they all have their own functions. Each organ in the human body consists of specific types of cells that carry out these functions. Since neuroplasticity happens in the brain, let's focus on the cells in this powerful organ.

Throughout our brain (and spinal cord), we have nerve cells known as "neurons." These neurons transmit chemical and electrical signals throughout the body. Also, these neurons are surrounded by "glial cells." These cells protect and support the neurons. The glial cells provide nutrients and oxygen to the neurons, and they also get rid of dead cells.

These cells are also smaller than the neurons, and they are greater in number compared to neurons too.

1. Neurons

Neurons are a unique type of cell, as they have a shape that differs from any other type of cell in our body. These cells are in charge of transmitting nerve signals from and to the brain, and these transmissions occur at a speed of 200 mph. Before we dive into the role of neurons in neuroplasticity, let's have a quick rundown of the parts of a neuron.

NEURONS AND NEUROGLIAL CELLS

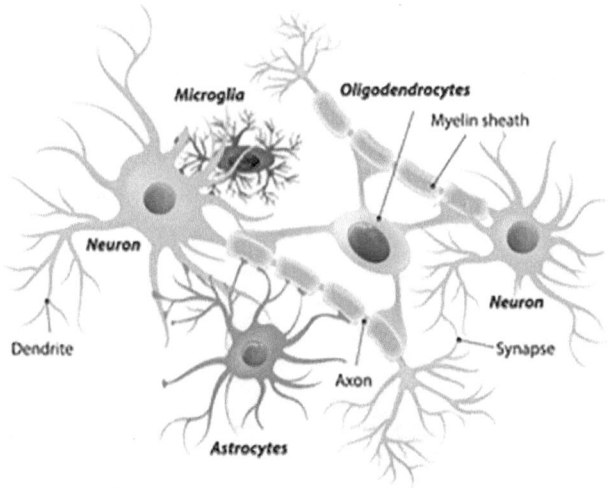

Typically, neurons have three major structures, which are the body, the dendrites and the axon. The body of the cell houses the nucleus, and this is where the genes of the cell are stored. The axon is a long and thin cable that carries the electrical signals called "action potentials" from the body of the cell to the other neurons.

Finally, the dendrites are short, branching fibers that receive signals sent by the other neurons. Neurons also have axon terminals. When information goes to the tip of an axon terminal, it gets transmitted to the dendrite branch of another neuron.

Connection between the tip of a dendrite branch and the tip of an axon terminal is known as a synapse. Then there is the myelin sheath, which provides insulation to the axon to help increase the speed of transmission.

Now that we've learned about the different parts of a neuron, let's look at the roles of these parts in terms of neuroplasticity:

a. *Role of the Dendrite*

When you have new experiences or you learn something new, this causes the formation of new dendritic branches, which look for the tip of one of the axon terminal branches. Over time, a new synapse forms, which then stabilizes the new information. Of course, this process may work both ways. As your memories or the information you've learned fades away, the dendrites tend to shrink, which in turn eliminates the synapses.

Remember that neuroplasticity occurs when the brain reorganizes itself in response to new experiences and information. There have been a number of studies performed to see how dendrites play a role in neuroplasticity. One particular study shows how neuroplasticity may help in the treatment of depressive spectrum disorders (Mateus-Pinheiro, et. al., Cell genesis and dendritic plasticity: a neuroplastic pas de deux in the onset and remission from depression, 2013).

b. *Role of the Nucleus*

The nucleus plays a significant role in neuroplasticity, especially in terms of addiction. Studies have shown that the rewarding effects we experience when we give in to our addictions are most evident in the nucleus (Marie, et. al., Transfer of Neuroplasticity From Nucleus Accumbens Core to Shell Is Required for Cocaine Reward, 2012). This means that the condition may affect the brain in a significant way. When we're able to curb those addictions (through the strategies we will discuss later on), we will be able to break our bond with whatever we're addicted to.

c. *Role of the Axon*

The axon is one part of the neuron that has been the main focus of different studies in terms of its role in neuroplasticity. In one particular study, they found that when an axon of one cell goes near enough to the axon of another cell to excite it persistently or repeatedly, a metabolic change occurs in either or both of the cells (Hebb, The Organisation of Behaviour, 1949).

Simply put, the more you repeat a certain thought or behavior, the more it will cause a change in your brain (as seen in this study and in other similar studies conducted about the role of axons in neuroplasticity).

d. *Role of Axon Terminals*

Since axons play an important role in neuroplasticity, axon terminals are also significant. When information comes into an axon, it gets transmitted through the axon terminal. When the information reaches the tip, it then goes to the dendritic branch of another neuron. As previously discussed, this connection between the two parts of the neuron is known as a synapse.

Axon terminals form offshoots into new pathways and new bridges. Basically, this is where "communication" occurs. This makes the transmission of information faster and more effective, which in turn helps with the process of neuroplasticity.

e. *Role of the Myelin Sheath*

In terms of neuroplasticity and the myelin sheath, there are different mechanisms involved. The types of experiences or learning you have may create complex alterations in the shape, size, amount, distribution and pattern of myelin. As you learn or as your brain tries to recover from injury, these alterations occur.

However, this doesn't change the fact that the myelin sheath is meant to protect the axon and provide insulation. The changes that occur in myelin production typically only happen because the brain needs them.

2. Glial Cells

The other type of brain cells is known as glial cells, or neuroglia. These are an important part of the brain and the whole nervous system, as they support the neurons. The glial cells provide insulation, oxygen and nutrients to the neurons while eliminating dead cells and harmful pathogens. These cells comprise about 15% of the total cellular composition of the whole central nervous system. Also, they're found in different parts of the brain and the spinal cord.

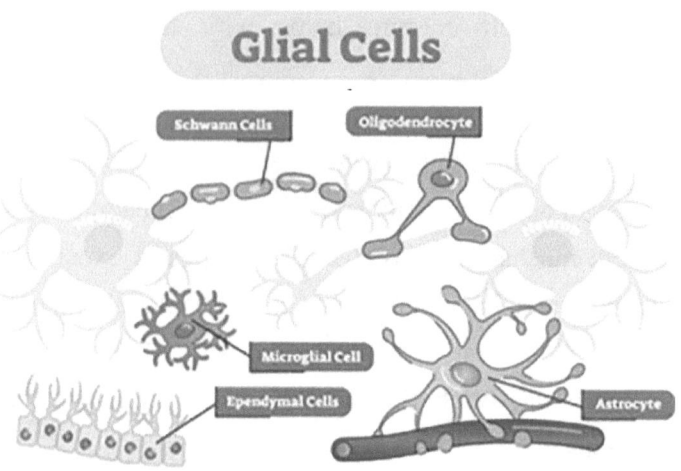

In the past, glial cells were believed to only provide support in terms of structure. As a matter of fact, the term "glia," when translated literally, means "neural glue." However, recent studies have shown that these cells perform various functions for the brain and for the nerves that run throughout the body. Just like the different parts of neurons, the different types of glial cells also play an important role in neuroplasticity. Let's take a look at the types of glial cells, what they are and their roles in neuroplasticity:

a. Role of Schwann Cells

Also known as neurolemmocytes, these cells wrap around other cells and nerve tissue to form the myelin sheath. These cells are an important part of nerve development, repair and regeneration. They also play a role in conducting nerve impulses, and in providing the T-lymphocytes with antigens.

In terms of neuroplasticity, Schwann cells have the capacity to stimulate the regeneration of the central and peripheral nervous systems. This is extremely important for when you have suffered an injury or you're trying to recover from some type of condition. These cells create a favorable environment for the axons to regenerate so that they can continue transmitting messages.

b. Role of Astrocytes

These cells are commonly found in the brain and spinal cord. They supply nutrients to the cells of the nervous tissue; maintain the ion balance in extracellular cells; regenerate and repair damaged cells in the spinal cord and brain; and support the endothelial cells. Recent studies have shown that the role of these cells is much more complex than previously thought.

Astrocytes have the ability to participate in the communication between neurons using their own neurotransmitters. They also uptake the neurotransmitters, then metabolize them. This means that the astrocytes can "overhear" the transmissions and change the flow of communication if needed.

One excellent example of this was seen in a study wherein the astrocytes were able to sense a specific transmission between neurons. Then the astrocytes "changed the flow" of the transmission by controlling how much transmitter the neuron released in the future (Min, Nevian, Astrocyte signaling controls spike timing-dependent depression at neocortical synapses, 2012).

c. *Role of Oligodendrocyte*

These cells, which are also known as oligodendroglia, provide support to the axons and nerves. They produce the myelin sheath, which surrounds the axons to ensure that they function optimally. On its own, this function already plays a huge role in neuroplasticity.

Even the smallest changes in the myelin sheaths produced by these cells can have a significant impact on the conduction of neural impulses. One specific study showed the importance of these cells (Monje, et.al., Neuronal Activity Promotes Oligodendrogenesis and Adaptive Myelination in the Mammalian Brain, 2014). You can think of it this way: The oligodendrocytes are the system that improves the flow of traffic along a roadway that is heavily used. In the same way, these cells ensure that the myelin sheath provides enough support and protection for the transmission of neural impulses to flow smoothly.

d. *Role of Satellite Cells*

These cells are also known as satellite glial cells (or SGCs), and surround the neurons in the sensory, sympathetic and parasympathetic ganglia. They are responsible for informing the body about stress and impending danger to prepare the "fight-or-flight" response. These cells are also involved in the regeneration and repair of muscles.

In terms of neuroplasticity, there was one particular study that clearly showed the role of the satellite cells. In that study, researchers discovered a way to obtain high-purity SGCs from the root ganglia without the process of digestion (Wang, et. al., A novel primary culture method for high-purity satellite glial cells derived from rat dorsal root ganglion, 2019). This shows the ability of the cells to regenerate or restructure, which is an important aspect of neuroplasticity.

e. *Role of Ependymal Cells*

These cells facilitate the flow of the cerebral spinal fluid (CSF). This fluid transports the nutrients to the brain cells and eliminates any toxic metabolites. In the V-SVZ zone of the brain (ventricular subventricular zone), there are stem cells as well as ependymal cells that radiate from the center and have several cilia for movement.

The stem cells in the middle of this zone create neurons that become your new memories. Since the ependymal cells facilitate the flow of the CSF, they provide the new neurons with much-needed nutrients so they can function optimally. As young neurons grow, they become stronger and are able to start communicating with other neurons in the brain. his is essential for creating a map in the brain consisting of sensory inputs.

f. Role of Microglia

Finally, these cells provide the nervous cells with immunity, engulf any foreign particles that cause harm, repair damage to the neural tissues and are involved in the signaling of extracellular cells. Basically, these cells are the central nervous system's first line of defense.

According to one particular study, any anti- or pro-inflammatory activity that is mediated by the microglia may have a significant contribution towards spontaneous neuroplasticity after the occurrence of ischaemic lesions (Sandvig, et. al., Neuroplasticity in stroke recovery. The role of microglia in engaging and modifying synapses and networks, 2018). This study shows the implications of how the microglia affects both the function and integrity of the grey matter in our brains.

Case Studies That Provide Evidence of Neuroplasticity

Neuroplasticity isn't a new concept. It has been around for some time now, and there have been a number of studies done that provide concrete evidence about it. Here are some of those significant studies:

Case Study 1

In this first case study, the incredible capacity of the brain for large-scale reorganization was shown in blind people, or in those who had suffered massive injuries (Siuda-Krzywicka, et. al., Massive cortical reorganization in sighted Braille readers, 2016). In this study, the researchers discovered that the visual cortex of blind people becomes active as they learn Braille reading.

Neuroplasticity comes into play as blind individuals learn something new. As they learn tactile Braille reading and keep on practicing this method of reading, the skill becomes stronger and the act of repetition causes changes in their brains. Although this may also apply to "normal" people or those who haven't lost their eyesight, there isn't enough definitive evidence to prove this yet.

In the study, normal adults who still had their eyesight were given the chance to learn Braille while the researchers investigated their brain activity using transcranial magnetic stimulation and fMRI. The subjects of the study displayed enhanced activity in their visual cortexes, along with their visual word form area, or VWFA. The results of this study show that large-scale reorganization is indeed a viable mechanism we can use to learn complex skills.

Case Study 2

In another study, a blind woman lost her ability to read Braille after she suffered from a stroke in the visual cortex of her brain (Hamilton, et. al., Alexia for Braille following bilateral occipital stroke in an early blind woman, 1999).

Studies that focused on neurophysiology and functional imaging have shown that the occipital cortex plays a significant role in Braille reading in early and congenitally blind subjects. In this particular study, a woman who was born blind suffered bilateral occipital damage after she had an ischemic stroke. Before the stroke, the woman was a proficient reader of Braille. But after the stroke, she lost the ability to read Braille. But at the same time, there was no change in her somatosensory perception. This is one case that supports other evidence about the plasticity of the brain and how it constantly changes depending on what we experience throughout our lifetime.

What Is Neuroplasticity?

Case study 3

This next case study focused on people who use sign language. Although they aren't able to hear, they're able to access the part of the brain known as the auditory cortex (Nishimura, et. al., Sign language "heard" in the auditory cortex, 1999). The upper regions in the temporal lobe of the brain are essential for hearing, and also for understanding spoken language.

The results of the study have shown that it's possible to activate these regions through sign language in people who are congenitally deaf. This occurs even though the normal function of the temporal lobe is as an auditory area. The findings indicate that for deaf people, the region of the brain that is normally meant for hearing can be activated through other kinds of sensory modalities. This is one study that clearly provides evidence of neuroplasticity.

Case study 4

In another study, the researchers were able to demonstrate the remarkable ability of the brain to rewire or restructure itself in response to a specific experience (Bonaccorsi, et. al., Treatment of amblyopia in the adult: insights from a new rodent model of visual perceptual learning, 2014). In this study, the researchers found that mice that suffer from amblyopia (also known as "lazy eye") were able to improve faster when they were given visual stimuli as they ran on treadmills.

Amblyopia can occur in people who are born with cataracts, droopy eyelids or some other type of defect that isn't corrected early in their lives. When these people reach adulthood, the recovery they experience is typically slow, and seldom complete. In the experiment, the researchers induced the condition in the mice by suturing one of their eyes shut for a number of months. After removing the sutures, the mice were exposed to a visual pattern as they ran on treadmills for a period of three weeks.

The "noisy" pattern the mice were exposed to was meant to activate almost all of the cells in the primary visual cortex of the animals. After just two weeks, the responses of the animals that were shown these patterns were already comparable to the responses of the normal mice. According to the researchers, this incredible response may have come from the built-in mechanisms of animals to keep track of any environmental stimuli, even from a certain distance. This experiment led the researchers to believe that activity actually stimulates neuroplasticity. And the great thing about this is that it can be applied to the brain and other parts of the body as well.

What Is Neuroplasticity?

Case study 5

Back in 1998, a landmark study was conducted about the ability of the human brain to develop new brain cells (Eriksson, et. al., Nature Medicine, 1998). This study challenged the prevailing theory, which stated that our brains were a very rigid system that didn't change. Since then, there have been other studies that have shown evidence of neuroplasticity, including:

- A study that showed that taxi drivers in London have a bigger hippocampus, the part of the brain that is involved in learning spatial representations and routes, compared to bus drivers in London (Maguire, et. al., London taxi drivers and bus drivers: a structural MRI and neuropsychological analysis, 2006). The study showed that the size of their hippocampus was directly related to how long they had worked as taxi drivers. This suggests that driving taxis may change and develop this part of the brain.

- Another study involved asking the participants to learn a juggling trick with three balls over a period of three months (May, et. al., Changes in Gray Matter Induced by Learning, 2008). In the study, the participants who had to learn juggling showed a significant increase in the V5 area of their brains, which is the area responsible for processing visual movements.

These are just some examples of studies that show evidence of neuroplasticity. There are a lot more out there that focus on the changes that occur in the different parts of the brain in relation to the new experiences, thoughts and learning done by the subjects.

As you can see from these studies, neuroplasticity is actually backed by science. The more researchers study this concept, the more they will discover about it, and about the incredible power of our brains to change and develop as we do.

Can We Influence the Process of Neuroplasticity?

Now that you understand neuroplasticity more, you know that the answer to this question is a resounding YES! We can, in fact, influence the process of neuroplasticity by causing mild stress to our brains, which, in turn, forces our brains to create new synapses. There are a few strategies you can employ to influence neuroplasticity. Let's take a look at some general strategies to start you off. These will give you a better idea of what you need to do if you want to apply neuroplasticity to your own life.

What Is Neuroplasticity?

Holistic Thinking

We've already established the possibility of changing your brain, as opposed to the belief held in the past that adult brains are rigid and hard-wired. Although it's true that the human brain is much easier to change during the earlier years, this doesn't mean that you cannot change your brain now that you're an adult.

One excellent strategy you can start with is holistic thinking. As you try to change something in your life, think about the big picture. This makes it easier to come up with your own exercises to recover from depression, injury, bad habits or any other kind of condition through neuroplasticity. As an added benefit, holistic thinking also has the potential to revamp your mental health as well as your life!

Doing Tasks That Require Different Motor Skills

Your brain is a dynamic organ that has the ability to change throughout your life. The next strategy you may want to employ is to perform tasks that require various motor skills. Learning and practicing motor skills can facilitate neuroplasticity. The more you perform these actions, the stronger their influence is on your brain. When this happens, the tasks become more automatic to you as they become part of your being. Then you can move on to other tasks that also promote neuroplasticity. Remember that the more you exercise your brain, the stronger it becomes!

Learn a New Language

Another way to change your brain is to try and learn a new language. This is one type of learning that can be highly beneficial no matter what your age. Previous research has proven that the brain mechanisms that are involved in learning new languages are those that significantly aid in the diagnosis and treatment of people who suffer from impaired speech after strokes, accidents and other similar conditions. As you learn a new language, this creates and strengthens neural networks in your brain that, in turn, improve your learning process. So if you want to influence neuroplasticity, try learning a new language!

Practice FLOW

FLOW refers to a state of consciousness wherein you become fully immersed with the task you're doing. You're "in the zone," which helps you feel and perform at your very best. Practicing FLOW also helps influence neuroplasticity in a big way. In order to enter this state of consciousness, you must have these conditions:

- You must involve yourself in an activity that has clear goals.

- The task you are about to perform must also provide you with immediate and clear feedback.

- There must be the right balance between your own perceived abilities and the perceived challenges of this task. This means that you should feel confident enough that you can handle the task you're about to do.

All About Neuroplasticity Games

Apart from the strategies above (and the others that we will be talking about later), there are also some effective neuroplasticity games you can play. But before going into these, you must know that most of the popular "brain training games" are actually ineffective. If you want to learn some neuroplasticity games that actually work, you may want to try those from BrainHQ.

BrainHQ is a brain-training system that you can access online. It was developed through 30 years of arduous research in the field of neurological science and other similar fields. This system was designed by a team of international neuroscientists who were led by Michael

Merzenich. Before you undertake the brain training programs offered by BrainHQ, you may want to prepare yourself. There are some neuroplasticity exercises that you can do in your life to prepare you for the more challenging games. These include:

- **Learning a new skill that takes you outside of your comfort zone.**

When you do the same things over and over again, your brain doesn't learn how to rewire itself. If you want to apply neuroplasticity to your life, try learning new skills that take you out of your comfort zone. Although doing this might make you feel uncomfortable in the beginning, you may start enjoying these new experiences as time goes by.

- **Take a walk and try to notice everything in your environment.**

One of the best ways to create new neural pathways to change your brain is through traveling. When you travel, you learn new things, especially when you consciously try to notice everything around you. Traveling doesn't necessarily mean going out of the country. Simply taking the long way home can count as traveling, and this can also provide you with new experiences.

- **Eat right and get active.**

It would be extremely difficult to apply neuroplasticity to your life if you're not at the peak of health. Your brain won't have the ability to rewire, reorganize or restructure itself if you lead a sedentary lifestyle or don't eat healthy foods. If you want to start training your brain, you must train your body first. Make sure you're healthy, and things will become much easier.

CHAPTER 3

How Age Is Related to Neuroplasticity

Neuroplasticity refers to the changes in the brain and to the structure of the brain that occur as a result of natural brain development, and in response to injuries or trauma. When neuroplasticity occurs in the brain, it comes with an increase in the number of synapses and neurons. The synaptic connections in the brain dramatically increase in number between birth and two to three years of age. This number is reduced by half during adolescence, then remains fairly static for adults. This shows that neuroplasticity and aging are, in fact, related to each other.

The brains of young children have the greatest plasticity. Their synapses and neurons increase in number dramatically even before they're able to start walking and talking. Between birth and the age of two to three years, the number of synapses in their brains increase from around 2,500 to a whopping 15,000 per neuron! This means that most toddlers have twice as many synapses as adults.

During adolescence, a phenomenon called pruning starts to occur. Here, the number of synapses and neurons in the brain that have been formed during childhood is greatly reduced. The elimination of these synapses and neurons happens based on all the experiences a person has through the years. People are able to retain the connections they use the most, while those which they don't use as much get eliminated. Right before a person becomes an adult, the number of synaptic connections he has between his neurons will have already been reduced by half.

In the past, it was believed that the number of synapses and neurons remain the same throughout adulthood. However, there has been new evidence that shows how neuroplasticity can still occur because of new experiences or learning. For instance, when you learn a new skill, this causes your brain to increase its number of synapses, which, as we've discussed, is an instance of neuroplasticity. Although as adults we don't have as many synapses and neurons as those who are younger than us, this doesn't mean that neuroplasticity cannot occur in our brains anymore!

What Does Science Have to Say?

According to a study, neuroplasticity can also refer to the final common pathway taken by neurobiological processes, as well as functional, molecular and structural mechanisms that result in compensation or stability for disease- or age-related changes (Smith, Aging and neuroplasticity, 2013). This is one study that clearly shows the relationship between age and neuroplasticity. The concepts involved here deal with the aging process, along with dementia, stroke and depression. The study also addresses a number of interventions, including cognitive and physical exercises (behavior manipulation), physiological factors (cholesterol, caloric restriction), pharmacologic treatments and the manipulation of the electrical activity and magnetic fields of the brain.

The translation between studies made in humans and in animals, as well as the cross-talk between neurologic and psychiatric disease is essential to move forward with interventions that promote neuroplasticity into the paradigms of clinical intervention. Although most fundamental research is focused traditionally on the "critical periods" that occur in the early years of development, more recent research is focused on the opportunities to apply or induce neuroplasticity in adults, or during other critical periods in the aging process.

This study, along with others, deals with the different aspects of neuroplasticity in terms of aging. There is still a need for more research in order to interpret any neuroimaging data that reflects neuroplasticity in the brain, as well as the conditions and specific points in the aging process or a disease process when interventions must be done to induce neuroplasticity. Through these studies, we will be able to learn more about how we can apply neuroplasticity in our lives more effectively, and in a more scientific way.

A Lifelong Process for Brain Development

In the past few years, there have been some fundamental changes in how we understand the capacity of the human brain. New studies have provided us with a more positive view of the brain and its potential to develop and change throughout our lives.

Neuroplasticity

The brain is considered a highly dynamic system that's constantly reorganizing itself. It has the ability to be shaped and reshaped throughout our lives. Each of the experiences we have changes the organization of our brain at one level or another. This means that brain development is a lifelong process. Just because you have reached adulthood doesn't mean that your brain will stay the same until the day you die. Neuroplasticity is an incredible thing, and through it, we can keep on changing our lives for the better!

CHAPTER 4

What Is Neurogenesis?

Another interesting concept that's related to neuroplasticity is neurogenesis, which is the birth of new cells. Neurogenesis is a phenomenon that represents an important aspect of neuroplasticity, as well as other important brain processes like memory storage and learning. It's another fundamental discovery that is still being researched today.

Neurogenesis is a fairly new concept that was only recently discovered. Back in the 1960s, Altman and Das were able to demonstrate neurogenesis in rats. But it was only in 1998 that the research team headed by Peter Eriksson discovered the phenomenon in human beings. Since then, other researches have shown that our brains have the ability to produce new cells even during adulthood, and that it's important for us to encourage this production.

The new cells that are generated through neurogenesis fit into two broad categories. First, there are stem cells, which have an indefinite ability to replicate. Then there are progenitor cells, which are more limited in terms of their ability to divide and renew themselves compared to stem cells.

Just like neuroplasticity, neurogenesis is also an important process. The importance of this phenomenon is clearly stated in a study about neurogenesis, cognition and cellular plasticity (Couillard- Després, et. al., Neurogenesis, cellular plasticity and cognition: the impact of stem cells in the adult and aging brain, 2011). When there is a continuous provision of new brain cells (neurons) arising from the neural stem cells of adults, this facilitates the execution of tasks that are dependent upon the hippocampus. This occurs because neurogenesis also reduces or blocks cognitive impairments. The study emphasizes the significance of memory and learning for the production of new neurons.

If you want neurogenesis to occur in your brain throughout your life, you must keep on performing or engaging in activities that stimulate your brain. Learning new things doesn't only mean acquiring a new skill. It also means that your brain is getting new neurons. Whether you're learning a new language, learning how to play an instrument or performing any other activity that stimulates your mind, this encourages your brain to produce new cells. Therefore, you should always try to learn new things, no matter how old you get!

Conversely, leading a sedentary lifestyle will have the opposite effect. This type of lifestyle doesn't just hinder neurogenesis, it also increases the risk of developing cognitive impairments. When your brain has a lot of activity, it doesn't cause damage to the neurons. Rather, damage is caused by inactivity, unhealthy eating habits, poor sleeping patterns, smoking, drinking alcohol and the like.

Neurogenesis vs. Neuroplasticity

To a lot of people, neurogenesis and neuroplasticity are the same thing. But this isn't necessarily true. Simply put, neurogenesis occurs when new neurons are created, and neuroplasticity occurs when new connections are formed. Neuroplasticity may occur if the new neurons created through neurogenesis are put to good use.

In other words, neurogenesis is the "birth" of new neurons, while neuroplasticity is the ability of the brain to adapt and change as a response to stimuli. Even though your brain is aging, it continues to develop through neurogenesis and change through neuroplasticity. One thing these two processes have in common is that they challenge the past beliefs that our brains don't change once we reach adulthood.

Although neuroplasticity and neurogenesis are two different processes, they work together in a synergistic way. For instance, throughout adulthood, new neurons are created in the different parts of your brain, and these contribute to your learning. And as you learn, new synapses are created between neurons.

Ideally, neurons should always be in a constant state of equilibrium. This means that as soon as neurons in the brain die, they should be replenished. But the generation or production rate of neurons depends on several factors, such as stress level, age, diet, neural activity, whether neurotoxins are present or not and more.

These two processes can be used for the treatment of brain injuries whether taken together or individually. Through the application or enhancement of neuroplasticity, the survival of the neuronal cells is ensured and compensated for through the reorganization of the brain and the rewiring of these cells. At the same time, neurogenesis can be utilized alongside neuroplasticity to regenerate or replace neuronal cells in a brain that have incurred damage or injury.

Where Does Neurogenesis Occur?

Neurogenesis occurs in the lower part of the brain's lateral ventricles, or the subventricular zone. But it is more evident in the hippocampus dentate gyrus subgranular zone. This is a structure that's located in the brain's temporal lobe, and is considered to be part of the limbic system. Some of the main functions of the hippocampus include memory, spatial orientation, emotional regulation, and learning.

Nowadays, there's widespread acceptance of the fact that, for adults, neurogenesis occurs in these parts of the brain. Also, the process occurs at a frantic rate, which means that there are a lot of new cells being born each day. Normally though, about half of these cells end up dying in a matter of one to two months. The brain cells that are born in the subventricular zone are transmitted to the olfactory bulb, but those that are born in the dentate gyrus are meant for the hippocampus.

In adults, neurogenesis may occur in the other parts of the brain as well. However, there isn't enough evidence yet to support this fact. There has been recent research that has shown that there are small, inhibitory, non-pyramidal interneurons that are being born both in the striatum and cortex. These interneurons create and secrete GABA, and may help in the regulation of larger kinds of neurons that create long-distance connections between the various regions of the brain.

How Neurogenesis and Neuroplasticity Work Together

For more than a decade now, neuroscientists have been trying to find out how neuroplasticity and neurogenesis work together to change how we think, behave and remember.

One particular study conducted at the University of Alabama at Birmingham discovered how neurogenesis and neuroplasticity work together (Adlaf, et.al., Adult-born neurons modify excitatory synaptic transmission to existing neurons, 2017). Through this study, the researchers discovered that neurogenesis and neuroplasticity work together by causing older, less-fit neurons to die off as the newborn neurons take over the existing circuits of the brain, creating healthier synaptic connections.

For this study, their focus was on adult neurogenesis that occurs in the hippocampus dentate gyrus. This part of the brain is the epicenter of the process, and is responsible for the creation of new memories, as well as the natural exploration of new environments and more. Specifically, the study focused on the newborn granule cell neurons found in the dentate gyrus, which should first get wired into a neural network through the formation of synapses (neuroplasticity) so as to stay alive and take part in the continuous function of the neural circuits.

As aforementioned, there are two main regions in the brain that can constantly produce new neurons through neurogenesis. The first is the spatial and long-term memory hub, or the hippocampus, and second is the muscle and coordination memory hub, or the cerebellum. Both of these parts of the brain contain a lot of granule cells that, incidentally, have the highest neurogenesis rate.

One of the most important parts of neuroplasticity is known as "neural pruning," or "neural Darwinism." As it turns out, neurons aren't "fired and wired" together into a network that can be extinguished. Instead, the UAB study suggests that the new neurons can help expedite the neurogenesis process through a "survival of the fittest" battle.

When neuroplasticity and neurogenesis work together, this allows the brain to create new paths for thoughts to travel on. his means that it's entirely possible to reinvent yourself completely, or even overcome past events that may evoke feelings of stress and anxiety. This allows you to live your life to the fullest.

How to Increase Neurogenesis

Neurogenesis is the process wherein new neurons are created or born in the brain. This process can reduce depression and anxiety, and improve memory. We've discussed how neurogenesis can work together with neuroplasticity to help you change your life for the better. Later, we'll talk about some ways to enhance neuroplasticity. Of course, it's also worth knowing how you can increase neurogenesis in your brain. Here are some tips:

- **Exercising regularly**

This is one of the most effective ways for you to increase neurogenesis. Exercise improves your memory and stimulates both GDNF and BDNF. Also, regular physical activity may increase the survival rate of newborn neurons, as well as the proliferation level of progenitor cells.

- **Getting enough sunlight**

When you get enough sunlight, this increases BDNF. Also, bright light has the potential to induce neurogenesis and lower both depression and anxiety.

- **Sleeping well**

Although the effect of sleep disruption in the inhibition of neurogenesis isn't completely understood yet, sleeping well seems to be extremely essential. When you experience sleep disturbances, this has a significant adverse effect on the proliferation of cells, and on neurogenesis as well. After experiencing chronic sleep deprivation, it takes about two weeks for adult neurogenesis to get back to normal levels. This is especially dangerous when you're also suffering from other brain issues.

- **Having frequent sex**

Frequent sexual experiences may increase the proliferation of cells in the dentate gyrus, as shown in a study on adult male rats (Leuner, et. al., Sexual Experience Promotes Adult Neurogenesis in the Hippocampus Despite an Initial Elevation in Stress Hormones, 2010). In the same study, the researchers found out that frequent sexual experiences promote neurogenesis, enhance proliferation of cells and increase the number of dendritic spines of the dentate gyrus of rats without increasing the levels of stress hormones.

- **Getting enough DHA**

This is a type of essential omega-3 fatty acid that is found in the body. You should get enough DHA, as it helps in the repair of cognitive decline, and is essential for the health of the brain, both of which are important for neurogenesis.

- **Avoiding sugar**

Because of the deleterious effect of sugar on the metabolism of glucose, it may have an adverse effect on neurogenesis. Raw vegetables and fruits may modulate the effect of sugar, so it's recommended to only consume sugar with foods that are rich in polyphenols and flavonoids.

- **Restricting calories and intermittent fasting**

When you restrict calories, this helps increase the expression of GDNF, BDNF and other nerve growth factors both in the basal ganglia and the hippocampus. Fasting has the same effect, and it also keeps the brain protected from oxidative injury and stress.

Aside from these, there are other ways to increase neurogenesis as well. The bottom line is that you must keep your brain healthy if you want to promote neurogenesis, which, in turn, leads to neuroplasticity.

CHAPTER 5

Why Your Environment Matters

The brain is an extraordinarily complex structure that always has something to teach us. As time goes by and scientists study the human brain, they keep learning new things that shatter our previous beliefs. One such discovery was neuroplasticity, which challenged what we believed in the past about how the brain stays relatively the same as soon as we grow into adults.

Of course, neuroplasticity isn't a new concept. But it is interesting to think about how our brains are able to change as a response to experiences, learning and environmental stimuli. This process isn't just a by-product of evolution, it has been occurring in us even when we weren't aware of it. Neuroplasticity happens both in the brains of children and in the brains of adults.

Our brains contain more than a billion neurons, which are interconnected by synapses. Neuroplasticity occurs when there are changes in the wiring of our brains. The strength of these connections between the neurons is modified according to what we experience, recall, think and learn. This type of neuroplasticity occurs as new synapses are either added or eliminated from our brain.

Apart from our own thoughts and actions, another factor that has an effect on neuroplasticity is our environment. Remember that the changes in our brains may occur as a response to environmental stimuli. Environmental enrichment is important when it comes to this phenomenon. Each of us grows and develops in different ways depending on what environment we live and interact with other people in. So if you want to improve your neuroplasticity, you may want to look into enriching your environment for the benefit of your brain. In order to improve your life, looking for a better environment may be the answer. In this chapter, we'll learn more about environmental enrichment and how you can use this to improve your brain's neuroplasticity.

What Is Environmental Enrichment?

Environmental enrichment refers to the stimulation of the human brain by its social and physical surroundings. The brains of those who are in more stimulating environments are most likely to experience neuroplasticity, along with dendrite arbors that are more complex and in turn lead to an increase in brain activity.

This effect primarily occurs during the development of the brain, but it also occurs during adulthood. When more synapses are created, there will also be an increase in synaptic activity, which leads to an increase in the number and size of energy-support glial cells. Environmental enrichment may also enhance the process of capillary vasculature, which provides the glial cells and neurons with more energy. With all these things happening, environmental enrichment may also result in an increased neurogenesis rate.

Several studies have suggested that when people don't get enough stimulation from their environments, this may impair and delay their cognitive development. Also, acquiring and engaging in higher education levels and environments that are more cognitively stimulating and challenging allows people to have a greater cognitive reserve.

There are some important components of environmental enrichment you may want to consider. Some of these are quite robust, and may have a specific influence on hippocampal behavior and neuroplasticity:

- **Physical activity**

This aspect of environmental enrichment is one that has been the focus of several studies and research. In one such study, the researchers explored the various aspects of environmental enrichment by dividing the animals into different conditions (van Praag, et. al., Running increases cell proliferation and neurogenesis in the adult mouse dentate gyrus, 1999). The researchers used bromodeoxyuridine or BrdU as their marker for dividing the cells. Through the study, they found that just placing a running wheel inside the cages was enough to induce the proliferation of cells in the dentate gyrus.

The researchers also discovered an increase in the number of BrdU-positive neurons both in the runner and enriched groups. This showed that physical activity improved the proliferation as well as the survival of newborn neurons.

Other studies (van Praag, et. al., Neural consequences of environmental enrichment, 2000; van Praag, et. al., Functional neurogenesis in the adult hippocampus, 2002) also support the fact that physical activity may positively impact neurogenesis, especially in the hippocampus.

- **Spatial exploration**

In addition to physical activity affecting neuroplasticity, when people are exposed to enriched environments, it may also improve their memory and neurogenesis. In one specific study (Freund, et. al., Emergence of individuality in genetically identical mice, 2013), researchers discovered that a vital component of an enriched environment is that spatial exploration that happens when animals live in such environments.

Using exploratory behavior as their measure, the researchers discovered that the mice that distributed their spatial coverage randomly over the whole environment experienced an increase in neurogenesis compared to mice that had a smaller and more stable spatial coverage. This showed how important spatial exploration is as a component of an enriched environment.

- **Other components**

Another component of enriched environments is the different types of learning that are associated with the hippocampus. One particular study showed that these different types of learning may promote neurogenesis in the hippocampus in animals (Gould, et. al., Learning enhances adult neurogenesis in the hippocampal formation, 1999). Of course, since this study was conducted on animals, it wasn't able to isolate the kind of learning that occurred and contributed to neurogenesis.

The social component of environmental enrichment may also have an effect on neurogenesis, especially in the mediation of olfactory neurogenesis. Researchers discovered this effect through another study (Monteiro, et. al., Enriched environment increases neurogenesis and improves social memory persistence in socially isolated adult mice, 2014).

A Study About Environmental Enrichment and Stress-Related Systems

One study focused on the effect of environmental enrichment on stress-related systems (Moneck, et. al., Effect of Environmental Enrichment on Stress Related Systems in Rats, 2004). The main aim of this particular study was to find out if environmental enrichment changes the responsiveness and status of the sympathetic-adrenomedullary and pituitary-adrenocortical hormones in rodents.

In this study, researchers kept rats in an enriched environment. These rats demonstrated higher concentrations of resting plasma of corticosterone. Also, they had bigger adrenals and an increase in their corticosterone release to buspirone challenge as compared to the controlled subjects.

Also, the rats that were kept in the enriched environment had lower adrenaline, corticosterone and adrenocorticotropic hormone responses. As these rats were exposed to repeated handling, this resulted in a faster extinction of the corticosterone responses. This showed that environmental enrichment may result in significant changes in neuroendocrine regulation, as well as bigger adrenals and an increase in adrenocortical function.

Other Studies

There have also been other studies that have shown how environmental enrichment affects neuroplasticity in a positive way. Let's take a look at these studies:

- **Education as an important factor**

Some studies have shown evidence that people with more cognitive reserve are the ones who have attained a higher level of education (Borenstein, et. al., Early-life risk factors for Alzheimer disease, 2006; Horr, et. al. Systematic review of strengths and limitations of randomized controlled trials for non-pharmacological interventions in mild cognitive impairment: focus on Alzheimer's disease, 2015; McDowell, et. al., Mapping the connections between education and dementia, 2007; Roe, et. al., Education and Alzheimer disease without dementia: support for the cognitive reserve, 2007).

These studies have also shown that, in addition to their education level, those who followed a healthy diet and maintained regular physical activity demonstrated increased neuroplasticity as well. These factors are components of an enriched environment, and they all contribute to the development of cognitive reserves, which are an important part of the brain's plasticity.

- **Early environmental experiences**

In another study, researchers focused on the role early environmental experiences play in the behavioral phenotype of animals (Salvanes, et. al., Environmental enrichment promotes neural plasticity and cognitive ability in fish, 2013). In the subjects' natural environments, these experiences affect the navigational abilities and anti-predator responses of the animals.

On the other hand, animals that have grown up and developed in captive environments demonstrate a reduction in their behavioral flexibility. In this study and others, results have shown that animals that weren't allowed to grow in their natural enriched environments had compromised neural development and neuroplasticity.

- **Long-term effect of environmental enrichment**

Although neurons are constantly being born from the endogenous stem cells then become part of the dentate gyrus throughout our lives, adult neurogenesis tends to precipitously decline as we grow older. However, a study showed that short-term exposure to an enriched environment may result in a significant increase in the birth of new neurons, as well as a striking behavioral performance improvement (Kempermann, et. al., Neuroplasticity in old age: Sustained fivefold induction of hippocampal neurogenesis by long-term environmental enrichment, 2002).

This neuroplasticity response may be important for explaining the benefits of brain pathology and function from leading an active lifestyle. In the study, the mice that lived in an enriched environment displayed adult neurogenesis in their hippocampuses that was five times higher than the mice in the control group. Comparatively, the increase that occurred in the neuronal phenotypes happened at the expense of astrocytes that had been newly generated.

This form of neuroplasticity happened within the context of relevant improvements in terms of locomotor activity, learning parameters and exploratory behaviors. The mice that lived in enriched environments also had a reduction in the lipofuscin load of their dentate gyrus, which indicated a decrease in nonspecific degeneration that's dependent on age. This means that the signs and effects of neuronal aging can be reduced by maintaining a challenging and active lifestyle, even when the stimulation starts at middle age. This stimulation has a sustained positive effect on neuroplasticity.

Environmental Enrichment Is Truly Important

Keeping your brain stimulated by having new experiences, learning new things and having new social interactions causes the brain to grow because of all the new synapses that are being created. Conversely, when you deprive your brain of these new experiences and bore it with the same old routine each and every day, your brain might actually start shrinking.

This is why environmental enrichment is so important. Your brain is always responding to how you interact with the world around you. The more complicated the interactions you have, the more novel your experiences are and the more synapses your brain will be able to create. This, in turn, increases your neuroplasticity, making the connections stronger and improving the overall health of your brain.

PART 2

EXERCISES FOR COGNITIVE FLEXIBILITY

"Any man could, if he were so inclined, be the sculptor of his own brain."

- Santiago Ramon y Cajal, Spanish Neuroscientist and Pathologist

Neuroplasticity

CHAPTER 6

What Is Cognitive Flexibility?

Cognitive flexibility refers to your mental ability to shift from thinking about one idea to another, as well as being able to think about several ideas all at the same time. Cognitive flexibility has two main subcategories (cognitive shifting and task switching), which depend on whether the change occurs consciously or unconsciously.

This skill varies throughout your life. Also, there are specific conditions that may cause a reduction in cognitive flexibility, such as obsessive-compulsive disorder (OCD).

Cognitive flexibility is an essential part of learning, and when you don't have enough of it, it may mean other things.

There are different ways of measuring cognitive flexibility. According to research, when you engage in tasks that require cognitive flexibility, specific regions of your brain are activated (depending on the task). Usually the activated regions of the brain are the posterior parietal cortex, the prefrontal cortex, the anterior cingulate cortex and the basal ganglia (Leber, et. al., Neural predictors of moment-to-moment fluctuations in cognitive flexibility, 2008). Other studies that involved subjects who had specific deficits have also added to the knowledge about how cognitive flexibility changes and develops within the brain.

The broader description of cognitive flexibility states that it is the ability of your mind to adjust your thinking from past situations to new ones, along with its ability to overcome thinking or responses that have become habits in order for you to adapt to new experiences and situations. This means that your brain actually has the ability to overcome habits or beliefs that you previously held as needed. If you're able to do this, it means that you are cognitively flexible. With this definition, you can see that cognitive flexibility is a lot like neuroplasticity. Both concepts support the fact that the human brain can grow, change and develop based on what you are experiencing throughout your life.

Aspects of Cognitive Flexibility

Cognitive flexibility is extremely useful because it allows you to adapt to new information and situations. Although there are several technical definitions of this concept, the simplest definition is that it's the ability of a person to shift his thinking as he adapts to new stimuli. To help you understand cognitive flexibility more, let's take a look at some of its potential aspects:

- **Deconstructing thoughts**

When you're faced with a complex problem or thought, you can deconstruct it into smaller chunks through cognitive flexibility.

- **Expanded awareness**

To some, cognitive flexibility refers to a person's ability to be totally aware of all the possible alternatives and choices in a given situation. For instance, if you're playing poker, you may be aware of the cards in your hand, as well as the possible hands held by all the other players.

- **Multi-faceted observation**

In some cases, cognitive flexibility can also refer to your ability to consider several elements of observation at the same time. For instance, you may be observing an object and notice its color, but at the same time you also observe its shape, smell, and texture. If you're able to do this, some consider it to be cognitive flexibility as well.

- **Transition "stream of thoughts" and attention**

Often, cognitive flexibility refers to our ability to shift our thoughts between several concepts. For instance, you may be with a group of people and someone starts talking about the benefits of following a keto diet. Then, out of the blue, another person starts talking about the challenges that come with traveling to a different country. In such a situation, being able to shift from one concept to another without getting confused is cognitive flexibility in action.

- **Updating cognition and beliefs**

Sometimes, cognitive flexibility also refers to updating your own thoughts and beliefs as a way of adapting to new stimuli or information. People who are rigid when it comes to their beliefs and think that they cannot change because they're already "set in their ways" are people who possess poor cognitive flexibility. Such people aren't able to update their cognition and beliefs, even when presented with new information or new stimuli.

CHAPTER 7

Exercises to Improve Cognitive Flexibility

Cognitive flexibility is a skill that requires constant practice if you want it to improve. Think of yourself as a lifelong learner that is always learning, re-learning, and unlearning things throughout your life. In doing so, you will start developing an "innovator's mindset," which allows you to easily come up with ideas while also being able to further develop and implement them as needed.

Cognitive flexibility is an important skill that's also related to neuroplasticity. To have this flexibility, you mustn't be afraid to reinvent yourself. The more you learn things, the easier it becomes for you to learn more. Of course, unlearning certain things can be extremely difficult, especially in terms of old habits and information that you have learned in the past and believed all your life. However, this doesn't mean that unlearning is impossible.

Remember how we talked about connections and synapses in our brains that can fade away into oblivion when you're not using them? Although some skills such as riding a bicycle or driving are never really forgotten, we might lose other kinds of skills, and even learned information if we don't keep practicing them. The good news is that when it comes to cognitive flexibility, there are exercises you can do to acquire this skill and improve it in the long run.

Before Beginning These Exercises

There are a number of cognitive flexibility exercises you can perform to strengthen your brain and help it grow. Whether you're trying to overcome a psychological condition such as depression, trying to get rid of bad habits or have some other personal reason for applying neuroplasticity to your life, acquiring the skill of cognitive flexibility will definitely help you out.

Exercises to Improve Cognitive Flexibility

Before beginning these exercises, you must prepare yourself. Cognitive flexibility isn't something you learn and then forget after you feel like you've already learned and understood it. This is something that you need to keep on practicing if you want to get better at it. Cognitive flexibility will be highly beneficial to your life. As you train your mind, you're also making it stronger to protect it from age-related decline and degeneration. With that being said, let's start with the process of learning cognitive flexibility by learning how you can best prepare yourself for it.

How often should exercises be done?

With these exercises, there is no "recommended" frequency for doing them. However, you may want to perform the exercises whenever the opportunity presents itself. As a matter of fact, it would be better for you to view these exercises as part of your lifestyle, and not just a routine you "have to do regularly."

As time goes by, the neurons in your brain that aren't stimulated will start losing their connections with each other. This is why it's extremely important to keep having new experiences, learning new things and performing cognitive flexibility exercises regularly. Think about it this way: If you never water the plants in your garden, they will start withering away until they die. And unless you nourish your plants, their roots will start dying, which will cause them to lose their ability to regenerate.

This same thing may happen to your brain as well. The nourishment comes in the form of learning, exercising and other forms of stimulation, such as having new experiences and interacting with new people. And it's never too late to start nourishing your brain once again. Recent research has shown that our brains have the ability to regenerate more than neural connections. They can also regenerate the neurons themselves! This is why it's so important to practice your skills and feed your mind continuously.

What are these exercises designed to do?

The main purpose of cognitive flexibility exercises is to stimulate your brain in response to new things, as well as to keep on challenging your brain. The exercises are designed to force you out of your comfort zone in order to promote both neurogenesis and neuroplasticity.

The exercises we will be discussing in the next section are meant to enhance your cognitive flexibility. They will be your foundation as you try to overcome a condition you're suffering from, or as you try to break bad habits that you have been doing all your life.

Exercises to Improve Cognitive Flexibility

As you're performing the exercises, you may feel some resistance. Don't be discouraged, as this resistance is an indication that the exercises are serving their purpose. The more you stick with them, the better for you they will be. Think of these exercises as your own way to strengthen your brain. After some time, you can start coming up with your own exercises that will help you step out of your comfort zone and lead you to self-improvement.

Most of the time, the problems we face in life don't have easy answers, which is why cognitive flexibility is highly essential. With it, you will be able to analyze the situation you're in and think of different plans to meet your requirements or goals. Having this skill means that you won't have to worry about freezing up or panicking when faced with challenging situations.

Also, having cognitive flexibility allows you to become more aware of your actions so that you can consciously make a choice to change them. This is an important aspect of neuroplasticity, as it helps you change your behaviors when you learn new information. With all these benefits and more, you can now see the importance of cognitive flexibility and how it will help you improve your life. Let's now take a look at some exercises you can start off with to enhance your cognitive flexibility.

Interpersonal Exercises

When you hear the words "brain exercises," you most likely think of crossword puzzles, meditation and other mental exercises that can help strengthen your brain and maintain its health. Of course, these exercises are very important. But in addition to these, interpersonal exercises are essential as well. This means that you must maintain relationships and social interactions in your life if you want to improve your cognitive flexibility and your brain's neuroplasticity.

According to neurologists, human beings are social creatures, and social interactions are a fundamental aspect of our lives. Throughout our lives, we play different roles based on our interactions with the people around us. Essentially, these relationships that we have define us. The more we maintain the roles we play as we grow older, the more we can maintain the health of our brains.

Plenty of research has shown how social interaction can have a positive effect on our physical and mental health. One such study showed how the amygdala, a region in our brain that helps regulate our emotions, develops better in those who have a more complex and broader social network (Bickart, et. al., Amygdala volume and social network size in humans, 2011). This shows how our social interactions may affect the functions and structure of our brains. This also means that our brains are naturally wired for social interactions to keep them healthy and strong.

On the other hand, when you don't have enough social interaction in your life, this may have an adverse effect in your brain. Another study that mainly focused on neuroplasticity and social interactions showed how patients who suffered from anxiety disorders displayed excessive neural activity in their amygdalas (Mansson, et. al., Neuroplasticity in response to cognitive behavior therapy for social anxiety disorder, 2016).

In this same study, the researchers found that this neural reactivity in the brains of the patients had the potential to be normalized through cognitive behavior therapy and other types of effective treatments. Part of the analysis of the results from this study indicated that a reduction in the amygdala GM volume was directly related to the relationship between a decrease in the neural responsivity of the patients wand a reduction in their social anxiety after they received treatment. This suggests that there is an improvement in neuroplasticity when social anxiety is reduced.

Neuroplasticity

When there is a lack of socialization in your life, it has an effect on how your brain develops. In some cases, the effects are so detrimental that they can delay brain development, especially in the early years of life. Without enough social relationships, you may start experiencing changes in your behavior, mood and the overall health of your brain. Other negative effects of a lack of social interaction may include:

- Poor self-esteem
- Depression
- Losing touch with reality
- Decreased learning abilities
- Decreased sense of empathy
- Increased risk of developing dementia
- Reduced resilience
- Physical manifestations such as inflammation, an increased risk of developing tumors, and even a shortened lifespan.

With all the adverse effects of poor social skills on the health of your brain and on your brain's neuroplasticity, you may want to start performing interpersonal or social exercises. These exercises are simple and easy to perform,

Exercises to Improve Cognitive Flexibility

and provide your brain with a lot of benefits. Here are some interpersonal exercises you can start off with:

1. **Talk to strangers:** Although we teach children to avoid talking to strangers, having interactions with people you don't know can be beneficial to your brain now that you are an adult.

2. **Read out loud with your partner:** This exercise is fun. It makes your relationships stronger and your brain healthier. Choose a book that you know you will both enjoy, then you can start reading out loud to each other.

3. **Take a hitchhiker for a ride with you:** For safety reasons, this is only advisable if you're not driving alone on a deserted highway. Allowing a stranger to ride with you opens up the possibility of getting to know a new friend who has tons of stories to share.

4. **Volunteer:** This is an excellent way for you to interact with others while supporting something you believe in. Volunteering helps you meet new people, interact with them and share common ground with them.

5. **Write letters to others:** Writing letters has become a dying art. But this doesn't mean that you shouldn't start this habit. This is an excellent way to share your feelings with others in a more eloquent way.

6. **Play with children:** Have you ever noticed how children play? They don't restrict themselves, and they seldom play by the rules. Spending some time with children during play is a refreshing experience that will strengthen your mind in many different ways.

7. **Join networking events and meet at least 10 people:** No matter where you work, you will have the chance to attend networking events. Take these as an opportunity to meet new people and interact with them outside of work.

8. **Join an acting class:** Even if you're not interested in becoming an actor, this is a great way to meet new people and strengthen your social skills.

9. **Do some acts of random kindness:** These acts won't just improve your neuroplasticity, they will also make you feel better about yourself. There's a special kind of satisfaction that comes with helping others, and it is even more fulfilling when the other person expresses his gratitude towards you.

Exercises to Improve Cognitive Flexibility

10. **Hug people for no reason:** Hugs are powerful things. The physical contact you share with another person has several health benefits.

11. **Talk to people who are older than you:** These people have wisdom and experiences that they can share with you. In addition to having meaningful conversations, you can also learn new things along the way.

12. **Interact with your pets:** People aren't the only ones you can have interactions with. Show some love to your furry friends as well if you want to improve your mental health.

As you can see, there are many interpersonal exercises you can perform to improve your cognitive flexibility and neuroplasticity. The key is to challenge yourself socially by doing things that are out of your comfort zone. Here are some other examples of exercises you may do:

1. Travel to a place you haven't been before.
2. Learn something new with your friends.
3. Challenge your own words and ideas by starting a conversation with other people.
4. Try being spontaneous when you're faced with social situations.

5. Mix up how you think and how you do things.

6. Interact with family, friends, acquaintances and strangers with an open mind.

7. Try to understand the thoughts and perspectives of other people as you interact with them.

8. Focus more on your real-life social network instead of your online social network.

9. Strengthen your relationships by investing time, effort and authenticity with the people in your life.

10. Join a dance class, a yoga class or some other kind of fitness class that can enhance your physical and mental health.

Exercises of Movement and Sensory Stimulation

In addition to interpersonal skills, motor skills can also help increase your neuroplasticity. Stimulating your brain through movement and sensory experiences may help form new connections and strengthen old ones. In one particular study, researchers found out how neuroplasticity that involves the structural reorganization of the brain occurred as a result of motor skill learning (Dayan & Cohen, Neuroplasticity subserving motor skill learning, 2011). The findings of this study demonstrated both structural and functional plasticity across various temporal and spatial scales that mediated motor skill learning.

In another study, researchers focused on the role neuroplasticity played in the motor rehabilitation of patients who suffered from multiple sclerosis (MS) (Lipp & Tomassini, Neuroplasticity and Motor Rehabilitation in Multiple Sclerosis, 2015). They investigated the different types of treatments for this condition, and found that learning more about the neural processes (such as neuroplasticity) may help in the potential recovery of motor functions of such patients. These studies and others show how important motor skills and neuroplasticity are to each other.

Of course, movement stimulation isn't the only thing that may have a positive impact on neuroplasticity. Sensory stimulation and sensory deprivation have the potential to increase neuroplasticity as well. There is growing evidence that suggests that sensory deprivation can promote neuroplasticity (Merabet & Pascual-Leone, Neural Reorganization Following Sensory Loss: The Opportunity Of Change, 2010). In one particular study that focused on auditory and visual deprivation, researchers found that the brains of the subjects had to cope with the sensory loss, and that neuroplasticity occurred as a result.

Neuroplasticity

Basically, the principle behind this study and many others is that neuroplasticity occurs during sensory deprivation. The brain undergoes continuous alteration of its neural synapses and pathways as a response to stimulation or deprivation that may have been caused by injury or experience. These findings show how important exercises are to promote neuroplasticity. If you want neuroplasticity to occur in your own brain, you may want to try these exercises out:

- **Close your eyes.**

When you're performing a task that's part of your routine, try closing your eyes while doing it. This opens you up to new sensations that stimulate your brain. For instance, while you're taking a shower, close your eyes. Feel the droplets of water as they meet your skin. Experience the warmth of the water, the smell of the soap, the steam enveloping you and more. You can feel all of these sensations better when you deprive your body of your sense of sight merely by closing your eyes.

- **Use both hands.**

One way to challenge yourself and your brain is to use both hands when you're performing tasks. This gives you a new experience of something that you're used to doing

Exercises to Improve Cognitive Flexibility

differently. For instance, if you're used to sweeping the floor or chopping vegetables with your right hand, try switching it up by using your left hand. Even simple activities such as this can improve your neuroplasticity if you make the most of them. Another thing you can do is to try writing with your non-dominant hand. When you practice this exercise, you might even discover that you can be ambidextrous!

- **Change your routines.**

This exercise allows you to have new experiences each and every day. Although following the same routine each day may strengthen the connections in your brain, changing your routines can help your brain create new connections. You don't have to change routines daily, all you have to do is switch it up once in a while to encourage the creation of these new connections.

- **Take new paths.**

Traveling and exploring are exercises that promote neuroplasticity. When you do them, you are able to see new things, have new experiences and meet new people. You don't even have to book a trip to explore or travel. You can do something as simple as taking a new path to work or to your child's school.

- **Try new dishes.**

This is one exercise that a lot of people enjoy immensely. Eating is a rich experience for all the different senses. So when you try something that's totally new to you, it's like feeding your senses as well as your brain.

- **Be the passenger.**

Most of the time we're so caught up in getting from one place to another that we aren't able to enjoy the drive. Instead of always being the one who takes people places, try taking the backseat for a change. As you enjoy the view, you can look around, talk to the other people in the car, and not worry about having to keep your eyes on the road all the time.

- **Learn how to play an instrument.**

Learning a new skill is always great for your brain. No matter what that skill is, the learning process helps your brain out in a huge way. And if you try to learn how to play an instrument, you're also learning a valuable skill that you may use in the future.

- **Learn how to type using all of your fingers.**

These days, a lot of people have jobs that involve typing and using the computer. Even while you work, you can improve your neuroplasticity by learning how to type with all 10 of your fingers. This improves your memory and concentration, and also makes you a faster typer!

- **Start growing a garden.**

Plants are an amazing part of our world. They come in different shapes, sizes, colors and fragrances. Growing your own garden involves a lot of different skills and experiences. From the time you plant the seeds to the time they grow and bloom, there is a lot to discover. The best part about growing a garden is that you can choose which plants to grow. And as you work on your plants, you're also spending some quality time outdoors in the fresh air.

- **Move your furniture around.**

Think about how you can reorganize your space by moving the furniture around. This task already gets your brain moving, all by itself. Then, as you start the process of actually moving your furniture around, your brain starts working even more as you see whether your plans will work or not. From the planning to the movements, there are many processes involved in something as simple as moving furniture.

As you can see, motor and sensory exercises and stimulation are so simple that doing them is a breeze. But as simple as these exercises are, they do help you forge new connections, pathways and synapses in your brain that make it stronger than ever.

Mental Exercises

Mental exercises are also important for cognitive flexibility and neuroplasticity. Since both of these phenomena occur in the brain, it's only logical that performing mental exercises increases them and promotes their occurrence. Without these exercises, your brain will start shrinking as the neurons and neural connections that aren't being used will start to fade away.

We've already established how recent research provides evidence of how our brains can keep on changing and growing, even as adults. But it is important to always provide your brain with opportunities to do both. We've already discussed interpersonal, motor, and sensory exercises, so now let's look at the cognitive side of things.

You may have heard the saying "use it or lose it." This perfectly applies to our brains and the importance of exercising them regularly. When neuroplasticity was first discovered, researchers found that we don't have to succumb to the effects of brain aging and deterioration. As long as we provide our brains with the proper stimuli, we can keep them healthy while encouraging their growth and development.

The concept itself is quite simple. As you improve on your skills, acquire new abilities or have new thoughts and experiences, the brain adapts to these by changing chemically, functionally and structurally. When you try to learn new things to improve yourself, your brain advances as well. So let's take a look at some types of mental exercises that you can do to help improve your neuroplasticity and cognitive flexibility:

- **Go back to school.**

As soon as we graduate from high school or college, most of us leave this world behind. But if you have the resources, why don't you go back to school to learn a whole new course? Not only will this give you an edge over others professionally, but it will also promote the health of your brain.

- **Learn a new language.**

This is one exercise that is commonly suggested when it comes to improving oneself. Learning a new language is very useful, no matter how you look at it. If you plan to travel to a different country, why don't you try learning their language first? The more languages you know, the easier it will be for you to communicate with people from all over the world. And as you learn, you form connections in your brain to make it richer and help it grow.

- **Talk to others about their hobbies.**

Learning about the hobbies of others is a lot like starting these hobbies yourself. For instance, if you ask someone about a hobby they're really interested in, chances are, they will talk about this hobby in great length. For you, it will sort of be like learning all about a new hobby that you never really imagined you'd want to learn about in the first place! Also, when someone talks passionately about their hobbies, this might make you feel interested enough to make them your hobbies too.

- **Read non-fiction books.**

Although fiction books are much more interesting to read, non-fiction books are extremely valuable too. These books contain a wealth of information about the real world. Reading non-fiction books can be very interesting and enlightening. And as your brain works to understand the information in these books, it is also forming new connections and pathways that make it healthier and stronger.

Exercises to Improve Cognitive Flexibility

- **Keep a journal or diary.**

This is an excellent exercise to promote neuroplasticity and cognitive flexibility. When you keep a journal or a diary, this forces you to think about your day, your interactions, your emotions and your thoughts in a more profound way. As you write down the words, you're also recalling the things that happened and how they made you feel.

- **Switch up your audiovisual habits.**

It's never a good idea to do the same thing over and over again. Watching the same shows and listening to the same music won't do anything for your mind. Instead, you may want to switch these habits up once in a while. This doesn't mean that you should stop watching the shows or listening to music that you love. Just open yourself up to new material that you might learn from, or that you might end up enjoying too.

- **Sign up for an online course.**

If you don't have the time or the patience to go back to school, the next best thing is to sign up for an online course. Nowadays, there are so many online courses available, and you can choose one that you're really interested in. The important thing is to start learning new things to enrich your mind and your life.

- **Ask a lot of questions.**

This is one of the best ways to learn new things and to understand the perspectives of other people. When you ask a lot of questions, you also end up learning a lot of new information. Whether you're in school or you're simply having a conversation with someone else, asking a lot of questions broadens your mind and makes you a wiser person.

- **Challenge yourself when you're faced with simple decisions.**

In situations where you're faced with simple choices, challenge yourself by choosing neither. Then justify this choice by explaining to yourself why you chose neither of the obvious choices. This exercise helps you look at things from different perspectives. It also helps you learn how to think of alternative solutions to a problem that, at first glance, seems extremely simple.

- **Create extreme associations when you're trying to remember things.**

This is a fun exercise that you can do no matter where you are. When you know that you should remember details about a certain person, object or situation, create extreme associations to help you remember these things. Create pictures in your mind that are so extreme that you won't ever forget them!

Exercises to Improve Cognitive Flexibility

There really are a lot of mental exercises you can do to keep your mind sharp. When it comes to such exercises, the important thing is to do things that make you think, and that challenge your previous thoughts and beliefs. After some time, you can start thinking of your own exercises to challenge your mind and make it grow.

Final Thoughts on Exercises to Improve Cognitive Flexibility and Neuroplasticity

In this chapter, we learned more about the relationship between cognitive flexibility and neuroplasticity. We discussed the different studies that provide evidence to support both phenomena. There have been several studies and research conducted that focus on the importance of performing exercises to promote neuroplasticity in the brain. These exercises are easy to do, but they provide a lot of incredible benefits.

So how do you apply this information to your life? We have gone through some of the best exercises you can use. Try performing these exercises daily and you're sure to see an improvement in your sharpness and the way you think. Of course, there are other concepts you have yet to learn. But when you start off with these exercises, you will be starting your journey towards changing your life for the better.

Neuroplasticity

PART 3

CONQUERING TRAUMA AND PTSD THROUGH NEUROPLASTICITY

"Among other things, neuroplasticity means that emotions such as happiness and compassion can be cultivated in much the same way that a person can learn through repetition to play golf and basketball, or master a musical instrument, and that such practice changes the activity and physical aspects of specific brain areas."

— *Andrew Weil, Spontaneous Healing*

Neuroplasticity

CHAPTER 8

Trauma and PTSD Defined

If you care for your brain and treat it well, it can be your most powerful ally. Since your brain is a part of you, it will always look out for your well-being. Our brains are naturally wired to help with our survival. They alert us when threats are present and ramp up our amygdalas so that we can take the appropriate action. However, the same trigger that helps us survive also makes it difficult for our brains to heal from trauma. As a matter of fact, the systems in our brain that keep us safe are also the ones that stimulate trauma time and time again. Fortunately, if you know how to break this cycle, you overcome trauma and other conditions such as PTSD.

In such cases, neuroplasticity again comes into play. In the 1930s, a behavioral psychologist from Canada by the name of Donald Hebb suggested that learning connects the neurons in the brain in new ways. According to Hebb, our experiences can alter the neuronal structures of our brains. And as we've learned in the past chapters, this is basically what neuroplasticity is!

Although trauma and PTSD can alter our brains, neuroplasticity can help heal us. When you have new experiences, your brain can start changing once again. This fact is extremely important in terms of trauma and PTSD recovery. But before we delve into this further, let's first look at the definitions of trauma and PTSD.

What Is Trauma?

The longer you live, the more inevitable trauma becomes. Trauma refers to a response to an event that's deeply disturbing or deeply distressing, and that overwhelms a person's coping ability. Such an event may cause a feeling of helplessness, which in turn weakens the person's sense of self, as well as their ability to fully feel their experiences or emotions.

Trauma and PTSD Defined

Trauma doesn't discriminate, and you can suffer from it no matter where you live in the world. It's important for you to recover from trauma because the more you let it control your life, the worse it becomes. Some of the more common causes of trauma include betrayal, loss of control over one's life, pain, injury, loss and abuse. The longer the effects of trauma stay in your life, the more difficult it will be for you to recover from them. Fortunately, it is not impossible.

There are two broad classifications of trauma. First, there's trauma with a small "t," which occurs when your life or bodily safety isn't threatened. However, when you experience this kind of trauma, you will still experience the symptoms. Your normal functioning gets disrupted, but recovery is much easier. Sadly, when some people experience this kind of trauma, they simply disregard it. But ignoring the event and all its unobservable effects can be perilous. If you don't process your trauma, it will keep following you no matter where you go and how much you try to cope with other negative things that happen in your life.

Then there's trauma with a capital "T," which includes extraordinary experiences that bring about extreme helplessness and distress. This type of trauma can be caused by a single event such as a natural disaster, an act of terrorism or sexual assault. Or it can be caused by prolonged exposure to stressors, such as child abuse, violence, war or neglect. Obviously, this type of trauma is much more difficult to ignore and overcome. When you experience this more intense trauma, you must seek recovery right away.

What Is PTSD?

Post-traumatic stress disorder, or PTSD, is a mental health condition that is caused by an extremely terrifying event. You can suffer from PTSD whether you experienced the event or simply witnessed it. Some of the more common symptoms of PTSD are having severe anxiety, nightmares and flashbacks. Most of the time, the person may also experience uncontrollable thoughts about the terrifying event that caused the condition.

Most of the time, those who experience severely traumatic events may find it hard to cope and adjust to their situations. But over time and with the proper treatment, they can get better. Neuroplasticity also has the potential to help in the recovery of this condition, but we will discuss this more later. On the other hand, if a person doesn't do anything about the condition, the symptoms might develop until they start interfering with the person's daily ability to function.

The symptoms of PTSD may begin within a month after experiencing the traumatic event. In some cases, though, the symptoms don't even manifest until months or years after the event that caused the conditions. More often than not, the symptoms caused by PTSD may start causing dramatic problems in professional or social situations, as well as in the relationships of those suffering from it. Left unchecked, the symptoms will start interfering with even the simplest of tasks. Generally, the symptoms of PTSD are grouped into the following categories:

- **Intrusive memories**

These include a recurrence of distressing and unwanted memories about the traumatic event; flashbacks; nightmares; and severe physical reactions or emotional distress over something that reminds you of the event.

- **Avoidance**

This includes trying to avoid talking or thinking about the event, and avoiding people, activities or places that remind you of the event.

- **Negative changes in mood and thinking**

These include having negative thoughts; feeling hopeless; memory problems; having difficulty maintaining close relationships; feeling detachment from friends and family;

losing interest in activities you used to enjoy; and feeling numb emotionally.

- **Changes in emotional and physical reactions**

These include getting frightened or startled easily; always feeling guarded; engaging in self-destructive behaviors; having trouble concentrating or sleeping; getting easily irritated, angry or aggressive; and feeling an overwhelming sense of shame or guilt.

Over time, the intensity of these symptoms may vary. But they're generally more evident when you're feeling stressed, or when you're reminded of the traumatic event.

CHAPTER 9

How Are PTSD and Trauma Related to Neuroplasticity?

The stress response of the body is a crucial protective and adaptive mechanism for coping with threats. But when a person experiences traumatic or chronic stress, it can result in functional and structural alterations in the brain. When you are exposed to different kinds of traumatic experiences, this increases your chance of developing PTSD due to the incremental growth of a fear network in the brain.

Neuroplasticity

There is evidence that supports how mindfulness can be an excellent form of treatment for people who suffer from PTSD. However, most of the literature doesn't really talk about the neurological changes that happen during the process of mindfulness. Research about the impact of mindfulness meditation on the brain in specific regions indicates changes in the function and structure of the brain that may account for why the symptoms of PTSD are reduced through it.

The deregulation of the areas of the brain that are associated with memory and emotional regulation are significant contributors to the symptoms of trauma and PTSD, along with over-stimulation of the amygdala, the brain's fear center. Mindfulness meditation can reverse these patterns by toning the amygdala activity down while increasing the activity of the hippocampus and the prefrontal cortex.

As a matter of fact, there are brain scans that confirm the fact that mindfulness has a direct correlation with a decrease in the amygdala's gray matter and an increase in the hippocampus's gray matter. Studies on neuroimaging have also shown that mindfulness can help activate the prefrontal cortex.

These changes in the brain that occur through mindfulness show how neuroplasticity can actually occur given the proper circumstances. Mindfulness practices can change the structure and function of the brain, which means that they can help in the treatment of PTSD as well as trauma. This is why this kind of treatment is becoming quite popular for these conditions, and for other types of conditions that occur in the brain.

Specific Regions of the Brain Affected by PTSD

PTSD is a condition that affects specific regions of the brain. Techniques for neuro-imaging such as fMRI and MRI have given scientists the opportunity to examine the brains of people who suffer from PTSD. According to their examinations, the three main areas that are most affected by the condition are the prefrontal cortex, the hippocampus, and the amygdala.

The amygdala is a part of the limbic system of the brain that helps you determine whether or not there is an imminent threat. In such a case, the amygdala sends out a signal that indicates danger, which in turn initiates your fight-or-flight response. Then, when the threat is gone, the same part of the brain sends another signal to indicate safety. When a person experiences extreme trauma, the amygdala ends up becoming hyper-alert, even to stimuli that don't pose a threat. So even if you're safe, this part of your brain will continue to activate your fight-or-flight response. When you suffer from PTSD, your brain remains on an activated loop, making you highly alert so you perceive threats no matter where you look.

In its hyperactive state, your amygdala constantly interacts with your hippocampus, the part of your brain responsible for memories. Brain scans have shown that those who suffer from PTSD have smaller hippocampuses, which is an indication of impaired memory in those who have experienced trauma. Normally, the hippocampus connects and organizes the different parts of memory. It's also responsible for finding the memory of a particular event at the proper place, context and time. But for those who have PTSD, their memories become fragmented because their hippocampuses have difficulty putting together the memory pieces coherently, differentiating the present or past, and integrating the memories they have from their experiences with factual knowledge and feelings. This is one of the most distressing effects of PTSD, and it manifests through intrusive flashbacks and memories. These memories and flashbacks trigger the amygdala, thereby causing it to stay in a hyperactive state.

How Are PTSD and Trauma Related to Neuroplasticity?

Finally, the prefrontal cortex is the part of the brain involved in the regulation of emotions, fear responses, impulses and behaviors. For those who suffer from PTSD, the prefrontal cortex is significantly less active. Therefore, it's less able to send signals to the amygdala to communicate that there is no threat, and is it unable to override the functions of the hippocampus as it triggers flashbacks and memories.

Our brain responds to trauma by changing. There are some parts that get deregulated, while others become hyperactive. This throws off the fine-tuned orchestration of functions that work together to protect one from real danger. Fortunately, these same changes, or at least the ability to change, can also help those who suffer from PTSD overcome their condition.

Learned Helplessness

For most people, when they have bad experiences, they try to do whatever is needed to change their situations. However, those who suffer from trauma or PTSD may also experience learned helplessness. This occurs when people feel like they don't have any control over the things that happen in their lives. These people simply accept their "fate," no matter how bad the situation gets. Since they believe that they have no control, they start behaving in a helpless way.

Learned helplessness was an accidental discovery by psychologists Martin Seligman and Steven Maier (Seligman & Maier, Failure to escape traumatic shock, 1967). They observed this behavior in canines that, through classical conditioning, expected an electric shock after they heard a specific tone. Through this experiment, they found that the canines stopped trying to improve their situation after being exposed to it for a significant amount of time.

Learned helplessness is also quite common in human beings, especially in those who suffer from trauma or PTSD. The longer people remain in this state of learned helplessness, the more difficult it is to take them out of this state. In addition to trauma and PTSD, learned helplessness is also associated with other psychological disorders such as loneliness, shyness, anxiety, depression and phobias.

Learned helplessness and PTSD

As mentioned, those who suffer from PTSD may also start experiencing learned helplessness, especially if the condition is left unchecked and untreated. When you experienced something horrific and it changes your brain, you may start feeling hopeless and helpless. When this happens, you start losing control of your life, and in the end you give up and just accept everything that happens to you.

If you suffer from PTSD and you believe that you're already starting to experience learned helplessness, you must learn how to address this problem. Although seeking professional help is the best option, there are some things you may do as well to help yourself:

- **Awareness**

Although it won't be easy, you must try to make yourself aware of everything you're feeling. This is the first step you must take if you want to proceed to the next one. As soon as you're aware of what's happening to you, it's easier for you to get out of the rut you're in and start helping yourself.

- **Change**

Now that you've made yourself aware of your tendency towards learned helplessness, it's time to make a change. For instance, if you realize that you're always having negative thoughts, make a conscious effort to think of positive things. Doing a reality check once in a while works wonders. After this, you can start making changes (no matter how small) to improve your life.

- **Take control**

As you try changing your thoughts and actions, you'll realize that you're slowly beginning to take control of your life. This is a crucial step to combat learned helplessness. But in order to do all these positive things, you may need the help of a strong support system to keep you focused on what you want to achieve and on the change you want to make.

The earlier you determine your tendency towards learned helplessness, the easier it will be for you to overcome it. Now that you know that such a condition exists, you can start reflecting on your own actions to make yourself aware of whether or not you're leaning towards learned helplessness.

CHAPTER 10

Conquering Trauma and PTSD Using Neuroplasticity

Knowing more about a certain condition helps you understand why it happens and what you can do to improve it. This is why we have defined both conditions and discussed their relationship to neuroplasticity in the previous chapters. Although it's recommended to seek professional help if you suffer from trauma and PTSD, applying strategies and exercises that promote neuroplasticity may help improve your recovery, or even make it faster. In this chapter, we will be talking about how you can conquer trauma and PTSD using neuroplasticity.

The most significant effects of these conditions occur in the brain. And since neuroplasticity is brain-related as well, you can see how it can help with these conditions. Being able to conquer conditions as serious as these won't be an easy task. But if you're able to do so, you will bring a new kind of hope to your life that you couldn't have imagined when you were feeling all of the worst symptoms and didn't know how to cope.

Overview

For those who suffer from PTSD, their brains have undergone a change because they either experienced or witnessed a severely traumatic event. We've discussed the three main parts of the brain that are most affected by the condition and explained the changes they go through.

But when it comes to the brain, what is done can always be undone. In this context, this means that even though your brain may have changed as a result of a traumatic event, you also have the power to change it back, or even make it better. This is the main benefit of learning all about neuroplasticity. Although human beings have always had the ability to change their brains through neuroplasticity, it's only in recent years that we are learning how to promote this change.

Recent developments in neuroplasticity provide evidence indicating that the brain is genetically designed and hardwired to heal by changing and rewiring itself after experiencing different kinds of trauma, including stroke, brain injury and others. Some research also provides an explicit explanation of how the brain changes. You can use this information to help you work together with your brain to support its development and growth after experiencing trauma.

Whether it's from PTSD or some other brain-related condition, recovery can be very challenging. Unfortunately, because of how difficult it is, a lot of people don't commit to their recovery. They just give up and accept that they have to live with their conditions for the rest of their lives. For others, they get used to a certain "lifestyle" that comes with PTSD, where they're allowed not to work, not to handle responsibilities and not to help others. The people around them are so afraid of making their conditions worse that they end up coddling those who suffer from PTSD. For these people, they feel like they're able to live an easier life because of the condition.

But would you really want this life for yourself? Would you want to feel helpless all the time? Yes, healing is difficult. It can get really messy, and a lot of times you will feel like giving up. In some cases, life will become a whole lot worse before things get better. In other cases, you will feel like you're making progress, then something triggers you and you feel like you're right back where you started. All of these things may happen when you choose to overcome your condition. So why bother, right?

Well, if you stick with your decision to heal, your brain will thank you for it. Those who give up aren't able to overcome their conditions not because their brains are unwilling, but because they are. It may take a long time for you to recover, but it's not an impossible task. How and when you will completely overcome your condition depends on you. The more willing you are, the higher your chance of recovering fully.

If you suffer from PTSD, you do so because of your experiences. When you apply neuroplasticity to your life, you can start learning how to use strategic, focused experiences to recover from this condition. At the very least, when you provide your brain with positive, new experiences while you start your journey towards recovery, it will give you an economic, balanced and positive way to change your brain through retraining. As you have these new experiences, new connections are created in your brain. The more you keep having these experiences, the stronger and stronger they become.

Soon, you will see how these experiences you chose to have are impacting your recovery in a profound way. Changing your condition means that you must be willing to do so. You must make a conscious effort to make this change. It will be difficult, but the benefits you reap will definitely be well worth the effort.

Creating New Neural Pathways to Conquer Trauma and PTSD

By definition, neuroplasticity refers to the ability of the brain to create new connections as a response to having new thoughts and experiences, or in order to heal from diseases and injuries. This basic definition of neuroplasticity shows how powerful our brains are, and how you can use that power to conquer trauma and PTSD. No matter what caused your condition, your brain can help you overcome it as long as you're willing.

To start, here are some ways you can promote the creation of new neural pathways to help you improve your condition:

- **Learn how to control.**

This is one of the most difficult things you will push yourself to learn in your recovery process. After all, most of those who suffer from PTSD and trauma feel like they no longer have control over their lives. But if you want to heal, you must come up with different strategies to help you gain control over the things that happen in your life. It's time to take back control so you can start moving forward.

- **Learn how to release destructive habits and thoughts.**

One of the best ways to learn how to take control is to start letting go of your destructive habits and thoughts. You may notice that certain things are always happening in your life. Each time you are triggered, you start acting or thinking in such a way that is self-destructive. As soon as you notice that you're doing this, stop and try to think of or do something else to distract yourself.

- **Activate your "warrior brain."**

If you want your brain to start changing, you must activate it. There are so many ways to do this, such as by learning new things, interacting with other people, having new experiences, and so on. These activities will awaken your brain. The more you exercise it, the more your brain will fight to recover.

- **Find balance and connection.**

You must also learn how to balance your brain so that it can start coordinating with the rest of your body and being. When you suffer from trauma or PTSD, you often feel disconnected to yourself. But when you start finding confidence in your ability to face new challenges, this brings back the balance and connection to your brain.

- **Step out of your depression.**

These conditions usually come with feelings of shame and guilt, which, in turn, may lead to depression. But as you learn how to strengthen your brain, you are also learning how to protect yourself and your vulnerable brain. Now it's time to energize your brain with positive thoughts and experiences. You may also try coming up with a life plan so you have something to look forward to.

- **Get enough sleep to restore your brain.**

When you feel restless, you aren't able to sleep properly. Even if you are able to get a few hours of shut-eye each night, the quality of sleep you have isn't good. You must remember that getting enough good-quality sleep is important to restore your body and brain. Therefore, you must learn how to sleep better by applying different relaxation techniques such as meditation, winding down, and so on.

- **Reconnect with other people.**

This is another important step in your recovery process. After experiencing something extremely traumatizing, most people tend to shut themselves off from the world. But if you want to recover, you must learn how to open yourself up to others once again. Start with those closest to you before you move on to meeting new people.

With all of these strategies (and more, which we will be discussing later), you can start creating new neural pathways in your brain. These pathways will help impact your brain for the better by changing its function and structure as a way to overcome PTSD and trauma. Now, let's take a look at other changes you can make in your life to help promote neuroplasticity:

1. Live a lifestyle of focusing on positive feelings

In addition to being a mental illness, PTSD is also a lifestyle. When you have this condition, you live each moment of your life feeling, looking for and identifying sources of fear, threat and danger. If you want to recover from this debilitating lifestyle, you must learn how to do the opposite. Try living a lifestyle where you focus on positive feelings. This will help you heal as you start letting go of your negative, threat-seeking thoughts and behaviors.

Whenever you experience a good or positive feeling, take a moment to explore it more, and connect that feeling to the present moment you're in. This is a simple but effective exercise to help forge new connections in your brain. As you connect a positive feeling to the present moment, this makes you feel safe and happy. This forms a new neural connection in your mind, which, in turn, tells your mind and your body that the feeling you have is real.

The more you do this, the more your brain will make changes that you need to recover from PTSD. So each time you have good experiences that give you positive feelings, focus on them. Live in these moments and you'll start living a lifestyle that's more positive than negative.

2. Mindfulness Training

Have you ever heard of mindfulness training? This is an incredible type of training that can help improve your amygdala, prefrontal cortex and hippocampus, the very parts of the brain that are mainly affected by PTSD.

Neuroplasticity

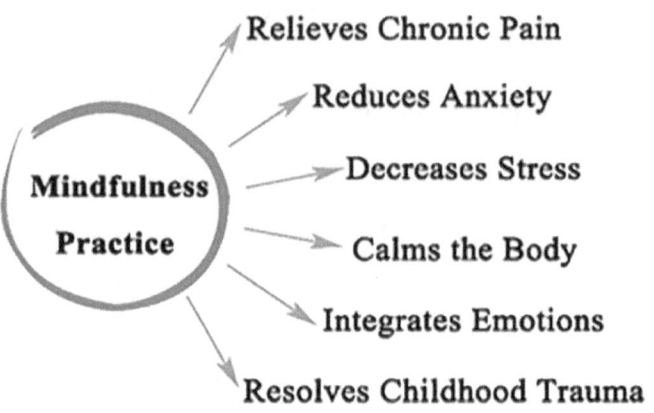

The design of your brain allows it to constantly change and adapt as needed. This means that you can:

- o Train your brain if you want it to change;
- o Measure the change; and
- o Learn new ways of thinking in order to change your brain for the better

For a lot of people, especially those who have been suffering from PTSD and trauma for a long time, it is difficult to understand how this is possible. But mindfulness training can help. Mind you, this isn't a quick fix that will help you recover overnight. Just as when you learn a new skill, mindfulness training requires a lot of willingness and practice. Through this practice, you can promote neuroplasticity to help your brain change in function and structure as part of your recovery. Through mindfulness training, your brain changes in the following ways:

- There is an increase in the cortical thickness or gray matter in the anterior cingulate cortex, which is associated with self-regulatory functions as well as the ability to examine attention conflicts and promote cognitive flexibility. in the prefrontal cortex which is mainly responsible for emotion regulation, problem-solving, planning and more; and in the hippocampus, which is responsible for memory and learning.

- There is a decrease in the size of the amygdala, which is the brain's "fight or flight" center, as well as the source of anxious and fearful emotions.

- There is either an improvement or reduction in the functionality of specific connections or networks. Specifically, the functional connections between the prefrontal cortex and the amygdala become weaker. This makes you less reactive, and it allows your brain to create and strengthen connections for your higher-order brain functions.

- One particular study also showed that there is a decrease in the activation of the brain's default mode network (Brewer, et. al., Meditation experience is associated with differences in default mode network activity and connectivity, 2011). This means that through mindfulness, you can prevent your mind from wandering frequently so that you can focus more on the present moment, especially when doing so promotes the health of your brain.

In another study, researchers found that PTSD treatments that are based on mindfulness training are providing a lot of promise for alternative or adjunctive intervention approaches (Boyd, Lanius & McKinnon, Mindfulness-based treatments for posttraumatic stress disorder: a review of the treatment literature and neurobiological evidence, 2017). The results of this study were derived by studying neuroimaging findings in mindfulness literature. The researchers also indicated that mindfulness training may help restore the connectivity between the large-scale networks in the brains of patients suffering from PTSD.

3. EMDR Therapy

EMDR stands for eye movement desensitization and reprocessing. This is a type of psychotherapy that allows people to recover from emotional distress and other symptoms that are caused by disturbing or traumatizing life experiences. EMDR therapy can be extremely beneficial for those who suffer from trauma or PTSD. There have been a lot of studies conducted where researchers found that most patients who suffered a single trauma were able to overcome their PTSD after only three sessions that lasted for an hour and a half. Other studies have been conducted as well where the patients overcame their conditions through varying lengths and frequencies of EMDR therapy sessions.

There has been a lot of research on EMDR therapy, and the American Psychiatric Association, the Department of Defense and the World Health Organization recognize it as an effective treatment for PTSD, trauma and other similar conditions. One of the reasons why this type of therapy is so effective is that it promotes neuroplasticity. This treatment has eight phases:

- **Phase 1:** This is where the therapist evaluates the readiness of the patient and formulates a plan for treatment.
- **Phase 2:** This is where the therapist makes sure that the patient has different means of dealing with emotional distress.

- **Phase 3 - phase 6:** In these phases, EMDR procedures are performed to identify and process a specific target. Here, the patient must identify a vivid visual image that's related to a memory, a negative belief he has about himself and any related body sensations and emotions.

- **Phase 7:** This phase involves closure, where the therapist asks the patient to keep a log for one week.

- **Phase 8:** Here, the therapist evaluates the progress made by the patient. This phase begins the next EMDR therapy session.

During EMDR therapy, patients can start creating new neural pathways and strengthening existing ones. In doing this, they're able to experience themselves in a new light, along with how they relate to others and the world. These new pathways created from the therapy help patients see things in a healthier way.

Can EMDR Be Done Without a Therapist?

The answer to this question is yes...and no. You can learn how to cope with distress and anxiety that are caused by traumatic experiences. If you're able to handle such moments well, this can help you recover. But if you want to get all of the benefits of EMDR therapy, this involves speaking to an EMDR therapist who can help you process your memories so that you can resolve them. The support of the therapist can help you in ways you might not be able to help yourself.

For instance, if you try doing the different phases on your own, there may be some memories that you don't want to process because they're too painful. But when there is a therapist involved, you will have to process these memories as part of your treatment. Therefore, you will be able to have a more profound process with a therapist compared to when you try to perform EMDR therapy on your own.

This type of therapy is an effective and safe form of treatment for those who suffer from PTSD, trauma and other distressing memories. Even if you simply start with EMDR therapy, you can always incorporate the strategies into your daily life for times when painful memories come up. Then, when it's time to have another session with your therapist, you will have a guide on how to process the painful memories that plague you.

Finding EMDR Treatment

When it comes to EMDR therapy, selecting the right therapist is the most important step. After all, this person will be the one to guide you towards emotional and psychological health. When choosing a therapist, here are some factors to consider:

- The therapist must "feel right" for you.
- The therapist must make you feel heard, validated and safe.
- The therapist must work hand-in-hand with you to help you determine the source of your troubles and how you can deal with them.
- The therapist must have proper EMDR skills and know-how.
- The therapist must be able to help you reach all of your treatment goals.

While finding the best therapist can feel quite overwhelming, there are a lot of resources you can use. You may want to ask around, especially with those who also suffer from the same condition as you. Or you can check out sites like www.emdrconsulting.com or www.emdrtherapistnetwork.com, which can help you find what you're looking for.

PART 4
CHANGING BAD HABITS

"If you believe you can change—if you make it a habit—the change becomes real. This is the real power of habit: the insight that your habits are what you choose them to be. Once that choice occurs—and becomes automatic—it's not only real, it starts to seem inevitable."

— *Charles Duhigg, The Power of Habit: Why We Do What We Do in Life and Business*

Neuroplasticity

CHAPTER 11

The Science of Habit Formation

According to scientists, habits are formed because our brains are always searching for ways to make things easier in order to save effort. If you keep doing the same thing over and over again, your brain will make these tasks part of your habits so your mind can "ramp down." Often, this instinct of the brain to save effort can be advantageous because it makes your mind more efficient. When you form habits, you don't have to consciously think about what you're doing, especially if it's part of your routine.

Neuroplasticity

When your habits emerge, your brain doesn't have to fully participate in the process of decision-making. Therefore, it won't work so hard, or it may divert its attention to other, more important tasks. Unless you consciously fight the process of habit formation, your brain will automatically work on it. Soon, your routines will become part of your habits.

If your brain has already formed a habit, this makes it part of your life. This is why it's so difficult to break habits, especially the bad ones. However, if you try replacing your bad habits with better ones, your chances of getting rid of them may improve drastically. Also, since habits are formed in the brain when you perform the same action over and over again, focusing on the neuroplasticity side of your brain may help you break those bad habits. If you want to make a change, you must believe that change is possible. And this is what we will be discussing in this chapter.

The fact is, habits don't really "disappear." When they form, they become part of your brain's structure, which is why you can perform those habits time and time again without having to consciously put in the effort. Unfortunately, your brain can't tell if the habits you have are good or bad. So when you establish bad habits, they remain in your brain just waiting for you to start doing them again. If you want to break these bad habits, you must practice avoiding them as much as you practiced forming them.

Myelination

In human beings, approximately 40% of our brains contain white matter, which consists of fibers that are densely packed. Myelin is the primary component of our white matter, and it is a crucial part of our brains. You can best illustrate the basic differences between myelinated and unmyelinated axons when you compare their performances.

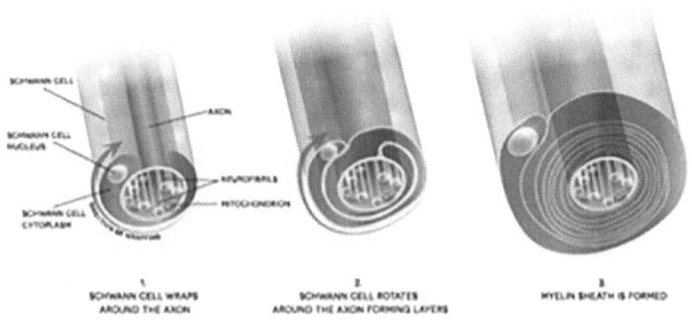

MYELINATION OF THE NERVE

Take, for instance, the unmyelinated axon of a giant squid. In order to perform at a speed of 25 m/sec, the axon of the squid must possess a diameter of ~500 μm. But the myelinated axons of mammals (including human beings), which have a diameter of just a few μm, can perform at exactly the same speed while utilizing 5,000 times less energy!

The process of myelination starts in our peripheral nervous system while we are developing in the womb. Our motor roots must first become myelinated before our sensory roots, and this occurs between the second and fifth months. At 11 weeks, the process of myelination starts in our spinal cords, then continues, following a craniocaudal gradient. Around the third trimester, the process of myelination starts in our brains. When this happens, it starts occurring in our sensory tracts as well.

Myelination that occurs in the pathways of complex association in our cerebral cortexes only starts after we are born. In our corticospinal tracts (the primary connection between our motor nerves and cerebral cortex), myelination caudally extends at the medulla's level when we reach 40 weeks. After birth, myelination continues, and the course of this process may increase when mobility is increased during the first few months of life.

It's important to understand the process of myelination, because it relates to our habits. Basically, practice and repetition cause myelination to occur in the brain. This process improves the coordinated activities that we do (in other words, our habits). Myelination speeds up the rate of the firing of neurons.

You may have already heard the saying "practice makes perfect." And when it comes to habits, this makes perfect sense. When you try to learn a new skill, you are promoting a change in your brain's wiring on a profound level. Several studies and research have shown that our brains can change through neuroplasticity, and that this can happen in children as well as in adults. Although there are certain things that children are able to learn more easily than adults, this doesn't mean that we can't learn these things too.

In order for you to perform a task, you require the activation of different parts of the brain. Our brains coordinate different kinds of actions, such as our verbal language skills, audio and visual processing, motor functions and so much more. In the beginning, a task may seem awkward and stiff. But the more you practice, the more comfortable you become at performing the task. This is because practice and repetition help the brain optimize for the task, along with all the activities involved in it. This happens through the process of myelination.

Myelination helps increase the strength and speed of our nerve impulses. This happens when electrical charges are forced to jump across the myelin sheath to the next open slot on the axon. The myelin sheath forces the electrical signal to "teleport," which means that it's able to travel at a much faster rate.

The process of myelination is a natural one, and it mostly occurs during childhood. Children absorb information at an incredible rate, but as we grow up into adults we can still continue to produce myelin in our axons. However, the process occurs at a significantly slower rate, and you need to put more effort for it to continue occurring. The good news is that the more you practice, the more you promote myelination in your brain. In the same way, the more you practice, the more an action becomes a habit!

Why Is Starting New Habits Difficult?

Think about the bad habits you have right now, those that you want to change. Now think about how to change them by starting new, better habits. This seems very challenging, right? But it's only "difficult" to start new habits when:

- You don't comprehend the structure of habits, and how to use this structure for your own benefit.
- You set yourself up to fail because you try to do too much right away.

So how do you start a new habit? Let's break it down:

- **Structure of habits**

Basically, all habits contain these basic components:

- **Trigger or cue:** This is what causes you to perform an action, and it can come from your external or internal environment.
- **Action:** This is what you do to either drop or adopt a habit.
- **Reward:** This is what your brain receives after you perform an activity you desire.

Most of the time, people fail at starting new habits because they don't understand their structure. In particular, they miss out on the last step, which is important so they can keep on taking action.

Why do you keep doing those bad habits, even when you know that they're bad for you? Most of the time, this is because bad habits are easy to do, and they are rewarding even though they are detrimental to your long-term well-being and health. On the other hand, good habits such as focused work, healthy eating, exercise and more require a lot of work, and you often don't get to experience the rewards until after you've practiced them for some time.

So when it comes to starting new habits that will be beneficial for you in the long run, you may need to help things along if you want these habits to stick. Let's have a practical example. Imagine you want to make exercise a part of your daily habits. You can make this more appealing by:

- Eating dark chocolate after each of your workout sessions.
- Rewarding yourself with a few minutes of a pleasurable activity (for instance, playing video games) after an intense workout session.
- Giving yourself a pep talk every time you're able to complete a whole workout session without taking a break.

As long as you're creative enough, you'll be able to come up with different ways to motivate yourself to keep on practicing the habit you want to start. This is a lot easier and better for your mental health than trying to force yourself to adopt a new habit and getting frustrated if it doesn't happen.

- **Setting expectations and goals that aren't realistic**

Speaking of forcing yourself to do things, setting unrealistic expectations and goals is a big no-no. Doing this would be the same as setting yourself up for failure, which in turn causes a lot of negative feelings. If you want to start a new habit, be as realistic as possible. You should know your own skills and abilities. Use this information to think of expectations and goals to set for yourself that make it easier for you to start and maintain the new habit you'd like to form.

- **Other tips to help you start new habits more easily**

Starting new habits doesn't have to be difficult. As long as you keep the structure of habits in mind and don't push yourself too much and too fast, you're more likely to succeed. Here are more tips to help you out:

  o Start out small, especially if it's your first time in a long time to start a new habit.

  o Make changes to your environment if you think that it's hindering your success.

- If you plan to start a complex habit, break it down and work on it bit by bit.
- Keep practicing the habit no matter how tempted you are to "take a break."
- Be patient with yourself and work at your own pace.

When it comes to starting new habits, you must also consider what motivates you. There are two types of motivation, namely intrinsic and extrinsic motivation. Extrinsic motivation is when you have an external reason for doing something. Conversely, intrinsic motivation is when you have your own internal reasons that drive your actions. With these definitions, which one do you think is more effective for you to start new habits?

If you answered "intrinsic motivation," then you're right. If you want to start a new habit because you're intrinsically motivated to do so, then the likelihood that you will keep practicing this action until it becomes a habit is high. Since you want this to become your habit, you'll keep pushing yourself until it happens. But if you're only extrinsically motivated, as soon as the external motivation is removed, your will to perform the action will go right along with it. Then you'll start thinking of excuses not to do the action, and in the end it won't become a habit.

Strategies for Forming New Habits and Making Them Stick

Psychologists describe habits as actions that you do routinely without having to think about them. This happens because of the meticulous ability of the brain to engage in synaptic automation. With enough practice and repetition, the brain hard wires itself to perform these actions so you don't have to consciously think about them while you do them.

Our brain is an extremely complex and powerful structure that has the ability to change depending on our behaviors, thoughts and experiences. We all have habits that are deeply rooted in our brains. Unfortunately, not all of those habits are good ones. We all have bad habits that we wish we could get rid of. But the best way to do this is by replacing them with new habits.

For a lot of people, changing bad habits is very difficult. But when you apply neuroplasticity to the task, you may find it to be a lot easier. According to neuroscientists, the best way for you to start changing your habits is by identifying your triggers. From there, you can start rewiring your brain by overriding your existing neural pathways. To do this, you must mindfully and consciously replace your bad habit with a good one. Sounds simple, doesn't it?

Of course, the actual process takes considerable time and effort. But as long as you remember that your brain has the potential to change, it becomes easier for you to accept the fact that you can initiate this change, making you intrinsically motivated to do so. Now, let's take a look at some strategies for forming new habits and making them stick:

- Identify the habit you want to break and replace with something better.

- Establish your purpose and value of starting the new habit.

- Understand the structure of habits (which we have already discussed) and how to change your brain (neuroplasticity).

- Set goals for yourself, and be mindful of them at all times.

- Focus on the new habit that you want to form.

- Take small steps towards your goal to build your confidence and strengthen your motivation.

- Stay positive and keep encouraging yourself, especially when you experience small victories.

- If you think it will help, find someone who can start the same new habit with you.

- Practice, repeat and then practice some more.

- Anticipate the early warning signs of your triggers so you know how to deal with them when they occur.

Changing Current Habits

As you can see, you *can* teach old dogs new tricks. Just because you have bad habits doesn't mean that you must keep doing them for the rest of your life. Once you realize that these bad habits are causing bad things to happen in your life, it's time for you to make a conscious decision to change them.

You must be willing to change these habits of yours and replace them with better ones. Of course, you don't have to change all of your bad habits at the same time. This is another way for you to set yourself up to fail. If you think it will help, write down all of the bad habits you have, then try to think of good habits to replace them. Then you can start changing your current habits one at a time.

We've already gone through the fundamental structure of habits. Now let's learn more about the habit loop to help concretize your understanding of how you can learn new habits to replace the old ones. Also, understanding the habit loop can help you learn how to break your bad habits by maintaining your rewards but changing your actions. Here are some steps for you:

- Identify your routine. For instance, perhaps you want to try and be a less negative person. Negativity is a powerful force that can exacerbate the effects of conditions such as depression, procrastination and anxiety. Therefore, if you want to improve your life, you should break this habit.

- Think about your rewards. When it comes to rewards, you must think of those that make you feel just as good or even better than the rewards your current habits give you. Working with the same example, being negative gives you an excuse not to try hard. Since you feel like you will always end up in failure, you avoid doing certain things so you don't have to feel like you're a failure. So what kind of reward can you replace this with? Rather than avoiding failure, you can strive for success. When you experience success, you will feel a LOT better about yourself. Even if you do fail, think of this as a learning opportunity for when you try again.

- Then it's time to think about what triggers your bad habit. In this case, what triggers your negativity? Is it a bad experience? Is it your own thoughts? If you're able to identify your trigger, you can be more aware of it.

- Now comes the hard part: changing your routine. One of the easiest ways to do this is by utilizing "if-then" phrases. Such statements provide you with clear intentions that help disrupt your existing routine. For instance, if you become aware of your negative thoughts, you can instead tell yourself, "If I continue thinking that I can't do this task, then I won't even try to do it." That way, you become more conscious, and you can choose to make a change in your routine.

- Finally, you should keep practicing your new habit over and over again until it replaces the old habit that you wanted to get rid of. When you follow this process, you'll discover how easy it is to break your bad habits.

Simple as the habit loop is, a lot of people aren't able to follow it. They end up getting stuck in one aspect of the loop or another, and when this happens, they get discouraged and then give up. Although giving up is the easier choice, you must keep in mind that you *want* to make a change in your life, which is why you're reading this book in the first place! To give you more inspiration, let's take a look at some examples of how you can use the habit loop to break your bad habits:

- **Too much snacking**

A lot of people want to lose weight, but snacks are just so hard to resist! To break this habit, first think about your snacking routine. Do you reach for snacks at a certain time of the day? Do you start looking for snacks when you're bored?

Think about how good you feel after you eat those tempting and tasty snacks. This, of course, is your reward. Now think of something that is equally rewarding. Perhaps you can do something else that you love and that can distract you from your snacking. Maybe you enjoy reading. Instead of reaching for those snacks, reach for a book instead.

Now think about what triggers your snack attacks. Most of the time, we don't really feel hungry when we crave snacks. Anticipate your triggers and prepare for them. The more conscious you are about how you want to lessen your snacking, the easier it is to break this routine and change it into something more productive.

- **Distracting yourself from work**

This is another habit that has become very common, especially with the emergence of blogs and social media platforms. When we get bored at work, we end up browsing through such sites until we realize that the workday is coming to a close and we have so much work left! To break this habit, think about your work routine and why you need to distract yourself from it.

Of course, it's more enjoyable to read blogs and look at your newsfeed than to actually do your work, right? So how can you make your work more rewarding? Why not flip the situation? Why don't you make these distractions your reward *after* you've done a task? You can break your tasks down and reward yourself after each of those tasks.

Then think about the things that trigger you. In this situation, boredom may be your main trigger. So you shouldn't allow yourself to get bored. Make sure you're always busy with your tasks so you don't end up loading those blogs and other websites that end up wasting your time. That way, you can become a more productive worker.

- **Staying up late**

This habit is particularly detrimental to your health and well-being, so if you're guilty of it, you may want to change this habit as soon as possible. Again, start off by thinking about your bedtime routine. Even though you don't actually have to stay up late, why do you end up doing it? Are you really busy, or do you choose to stay up late because you're doing things that aren't really important?

Those things you do that prevent you from sleeping early may feel rewarding to you in the moment, but in the long run your lack of sleep is causing adverse effects to your health. Sleep can actually be extremely rewarding. If you sleep at the right time and wake up at the right time, you'll start feeling more relaxed and energized each day. This can be your reward if you so choose.

With that in mind, it's time to start building a different bedtime routine, one that will allow you to go to bed earlier. Get rid of the things that make you stay up late. Turn of your television, smartphone and other gadgets that may be the cause of your late nights. Replace them with meditation and other relaxing activities that will help you relax and drift off at a more reasonable hour.

These are just a few examples of how you can use the habit loop to break your bad habits and change them to better ones. Now try to think of one or two bad habits you would like to change right now, along with some steps to do so. Here are a few lines for you to write down your own plans:

_____
_____
_____
_____
_____
_____
_____

Habit Formation and Neuroplasticity

How you live your life will determine what your brain will look like. Whenever you form a new habit, this habit will represent itself in your brain. Essentially, this is neuroplasticity in action, and it plays an important role in the formation of habits.

When you do something regularly, whether it's something bad or good, your brain will create neural connections. This means that when you either break a habit or create a new one, neuroplasticity comes into play. When a new habit is formed, the brain releases a chemical known as dopamine that makes you feel happy and good. This chemical is important for the creation of neural connections, as well as strengthening the existing neural connections that reinforce the habit you have formed. This is why changing a habit also means changing your brain.

Although it's not that easy to break bad habits, it is not impossible. The process of breaking, changing and forming habits causes a change in the brain's structure. This creates alternate pathways in the brain. But you must put a lot of intentional thought and effort into these habits in order for your brain to make the required changes.

PART 5
ELIMINATING DEPRESSION

"Because of the power of neuroplasticity, you can, in fact, reframe your world and rewire your brain so that you are more objective. You have the power to see things as they are so that you can respond thoughtfully, deliberately, and effectively to everything you experience."

- *Elizabeth Thornton*

Neuroplasticity

CHAPTER 12

Brains Suffering From Depression

Depression is a mood disorder that has an effect on how a person behaves, thinks and feels. This condition causes the person to feel hopeless or sad, and these episodes can last anywhere from a couple of days to a couple of years. It's important to note that depression isn't the same as feeling sad, upset or disappointed at some point during the day. It's an actual disorder that needs appropriate treatment.

Depression can vary in severity depending on the experiences of the person, his environment and other factors. The most common symptoms of depression include:

- Feelings of hopelessness and sadness that don't go away
- A lack of interest in doing things, even the things that you used to enjoy
- An increase or decrease in your appetite, along with extreme weight loss or weight gain
- Sleeping too little or too much
- Fatigue and restlessness
- Inappropriate or excessive feelings of worthlessness or guilt
- Difficulty thinking, concentrating and making decisions
- Multiple and frequent thoughts of suicide or death
- Suicide attempts

Although researchers don't know exactly what causes depression, there are some factors that may play a role in the development of the condition including stress, genetics, hormonal imbalances, and biochemical reactions.

As with PTSD and trauma, the areas affected by the brain are the amygdala, the hippocampus and the prefrontal cortex. Most experts believe that high levels of cortisol play the most significant role in the chemical and physical changes that occur in the brains of those who suffer from depression. Other studies have also shown that the thalamus and frontal cortex of the brain may be affected by this condition.

Normal Brain vs. Depressed Brain

Depression is a real condition that shouldn't be easily dismissed. Unfortunately, some people don't understand how this condition differs from just having a bad day or a bad mood. Although the causes of this condition aren't definitively established, studies have shown that the brains of those who are depressed differ from normal brains. In particular, a study conducted in London's University College shed new light on these differences (Lawson, et. al., Disrupted habenula function in major depression, 2017).

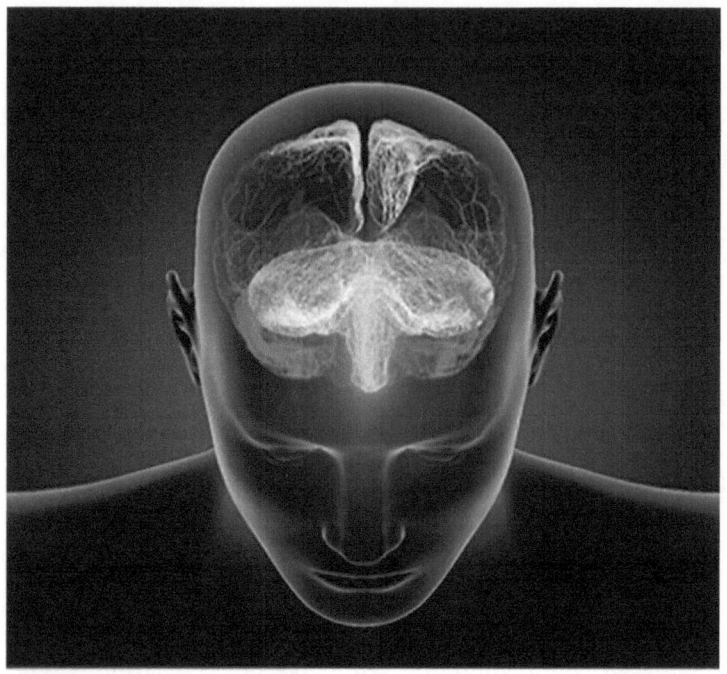

In this study, the researchers compared the MRI brain scans of people who suffer from depression with the brain scans of people who have never exhibited the symptoms of depression in their lives. The major finding of this study was that there was a significant difference between the activity of the habenula, which is the part of the brain involved in sleep cycles, learning, stress responses and other important functions.

The researchers also discovered physical differences in the brains of the subjects, although not in the average size of their habenula. However, those subjects who had a habenula with a smaller size demonstrated more symptoms of a condition known as anhedonia, wherein you lack the ability to experience the pleasures of life. The bottom line of this study was that the habenula may play an important role in depression, particularly in helping those who suffer from it avoid dwelling on unpleasant memories or thoughts.

Decreased Neuroplasticity

Neuroscience research that has been conducted on the biological aspect of mood disorders such as depression shows how widespread and profound the effect of the condition is on the human brain. Although there is a high likelihood that depression is triggered when there is a disruption in the activity of specific circuits of the brain, the condition also influences the cellular and biochemical balance of the different parts of the brain.

For those who suffer from depression, their brains seem impoverished. There is a disruption of the normal growth factors, the balance of glial cells that support the neurons is thrown off and there is a diminution of their capacity for neuroplasticity.

Depression causes damage to the brain, and the longer it stays with the person, the more severe the condition gets.

Subsequently, the process affects more and more parts of the brain. This is why depression comes with a wide range of symptoms. Your thoughts, hormones, feelings, motivations, social interactions and hormonal functions get disrupted. This is also why it's extremely difficult to treat recurrent and severe depression.

Although depression can decrease neuroplasticity, you can also use neuroplasticity to help combat this condition. To do this, you must activate the proper circuits of the brain that promote healthy pleasure, joy and other positive emotions. This makes your brain stronger and more well-protected against the condition. We will discuss the "how" of this in the next chapter.

PET Scans of Depressed Brain

People who suffer from depression have some specific and common structural brain irregularities that can only be seen through imaging scans. One particular study conducted at China's Sichuan University came up with a major finding about this (Jiang & Zhao, Microstructural brain abnormalities in medication-free patients with major depressive disorder: A systematic review and meta-analysis of diffusion tensor imaging, 2016).

Brains Suffering From Depression

The researchers examined high-resolution MRI scans of people who suffered from depression and social anxiety, and those who didn't have any mental conditions. They searched for differences, specifically in the grey matter of the brain. They examined the thickness of their cerebral cortex, which is the part of the brain responsible for most of the information processing functions.

In another study related to depression, researchers found out that brain imaging can help predict suicide. The researchers who led this study were Marcel Just from Carnegie Mellon University and David Brent from the University of Pittsburgh. Together, they developed a promising and innovative approach to identifying individuals who have a tendency towards suicide by analyzing the changes in their brains.

Such studies and more show how MRI can help researchers identify depression and all its symptoms and effects in those who suffer from the condition. In terms of PET scans, those who suffer from depression show an increase of green and blue colors, along with a decrease in yellow and white colors, which indicates a decrease in the overall brain activity caused by the condition.

CHAPTER 13

Using the Principle of Repetition to Eliminate Depression

We've discussed how repetition and practice can promote neuroplasticity for the purpose of breaking bad habits and learning new ones. This concept is very important because you can also use it to help eliminate depression. It's important to remember that the strategies of repetition differ from merely "thinking positively." When you keep on repeating these strategies, physical connections are created and strengthened in your brain, which causes changes in its function and structure.

When it comes to repetition, how focused you are and what you think or do repetitively are important. For instance, if you always have positive thoughts in your mind, you're likely to feel better compared to when you always dwell on negative thoughts. Thinking about something repetitively is like performing a "mental rehearsal" that makes those thoughts come to mind more easily in the future.

Also, you must consider your repetitive thinking style. For instance, you can focus on information that is "negative" but use this information in a manner that will prove helpful to you. If you are focused on a failure that happened in your life, you can shift your style of thinking and keep repeating how you could have improved the situation so you can succeed in the future.

The Trouble with Positive Thinking

We have all heard of positive thinking, and a lot of people rely on this to make their lives better. Although positive thinking may work for some people, you shouldn't rely on it too much because, just like everything else in this world, it also has a downside.

Yes, having positive thoughts and repeating them to yourself over and over again can help promote neuroplasticity. But when it comes to positive thinking and depression, the former might place you more at risk for the latter, especially if you only rely on positive thinking and nothing else. Here are some of the disadvantages of positive thinking:

- You might end up having unrealistic expectations about your life, which may backfire on you.

- It's impossible for anyone to become an optimist just like that.

- It may lead to deluded optimism, which is a lot worse than realistic pessimism.

On occasion, positive thinking can be beneficial. But if you want to promote neuroplasticity and improve your life, then you should do more than just think positively.

The Power of Words

Neuroplasticity is a complex process. There are many different exercises you can perform to promote it if you want to make a change for the better. Apart from your actions, thoughts and experiences, words can also have a significant effect on neuroplasticity, and this mainly comes

Using the Principle of Repetition to Eliminate Depression

in the form of affirmations. Let's learn more about this concept.

1. What Do You Expose Your Brain To?

Have you ever asked yourself this question? Words are a powerful thing. Whatever you say to yourself goes into your brain. This means that if you want to change your brain for the better, you must try to provide as many affirmations to it as you can. Combining these with the other exercises and strategies will definitely help produce changes in your brain that can help you overcome depression, your bad habits and any other conditions you're struggling with now.

2. The Power of Affirmations

Unlike neuroplasticity, affirmations aren't a new concept. Simply put, affirmations are phrases or statements you say to yourself repeatedly. You can create your own affirmations depending on what you want to improve in your life, or you can find affirmations online that fit into your current situation. Although affirmations won't solve your problems, practicing them regularly can help rewire and reshape your brain to cause the behavioral changes you want to incorporate in your life.

Neuroplasticity

Try to remember the exercises we talked about in the previous chapters. For instance, trying to improve your cognitive flexibility and neuroplasticity by performing interpersonal exercises. When you suffer from depression, interacting with other people can be a huge challenge. So how can you help move things along?

For such a situation, you can come up with affirmations like "I enjoy meeting new people," "I love reconnecting with old friends," "Meeting new people is fun!" or something similar. When you keep saying these statements to yourself over and over again, a couple of times each day, your brain will start believing them. Then, when you're faced with a situation where you are about to meet new people or reconnect with old friends, you'll find that it's a lot easier.

This is just one example of how affirmations work. You can also use affirmations to change your bad habits, to overcome the issues you're dealing with because of your depression and so much more. The key is to come up with the appropriate statements and keep on repeating them to yourself until you believe that they are true. Then it becomes easier to act on the statements and make them a reality.

3. Affirmations to Eliminate Depression

In 2010, there was promising research conducted at Arizona State University that demonstrated how affirmations can supplement the treatment of patients who suffered from depression. In fact, for some of the patients, affirmations were the most influential aspect of their process of recovery. This means that your belief and willingness to embrace the affirmations you keep repeating to yourself increases the chance of them making a huge positive impact on your life.

As long as you pair these affirmations with actions and conscious effort, you can make a positive impact on your condition. If you suffer from depression, here are some powerful affirmations you may want to start saying to yourself:

- I am a strong person!
- I love myself!
- I only allow loving and healthy relationships into my life.
- Life wants what's best for me.
- I am comfortable and connected with all kinds of people.

- I find joy in life's simple pleasures.
- My feelings matter, so I focus on things that make me feel good!
- The challenges I face bring better opportunities with them.
- I am positive and peaceful.
- I am in control of my life.

As mentioned, you can also come up with your own affirmations. Just make sure that they are specific and personal, and that the statements are focused on the present.

Stimulating Our Brains to Encode Joy

When it comes to depression and the brain, possibly the best way to protect yourself from developing the condition is to stimulate your brain to encode joy. Remember that depression causes structural and functional changes in the brain. So if you make sure that the circuitry of your brain is stimulated by positivity, joy and pleasure, this can help combat the effects of depression.

More than your thoughts, if you perform activities or have experiences that naturally activate the circuits of your brain that encode joy, these circuits will start transmitting the message to the other parts of the brain to enrich them and

Using the Principle of Repetition to Eliminate Depression

protect you against depression. With that being said, here are some activities you can do to activate feelings of pleasure and enjoyment:

- Take on a challenging activity that you think is really fun and stick with it until you gain proficiency.
- Actively search for joy by finding different sources of inspiration.
- Engage in activities that feel like play.
- Rather than ignoring sad experiences, deal with them so they don't block your joyful feelings.
- Honor yourself frequently and consciously.
- Once in a while, take a break from your normal daily routine.
- Use affirmations often, and focus on what they mean in your life.
- When thinking of goals in life, make happiness one of them.
- Do some self-reflection and find out what really makes you feel happy so you can go after it.
- Make happiness your priority.

- Take the time to "smell the roses" and appreciate the small things in life.

- Use your time wisely. Make sure a part of it is for doing something that makes you happy.

- Think happy thoughts!

- Once in a while, spend your money on something that you really like.

- Meet new people with the purpose of falling in love.

- Come up with a back-up plan, especially when you're planning to do something that means a lot to you.

- When you're doing something enjoyable or pleasurable, try to find the purpose of the activity to make it much more meaningful.

- Spend quality time with those who make you feel good.

- Disconnect from technology and explore the real world once in a while.

- Be kind to other people.

- Designate one day each week for fun or relaxing activities.
- Breathe deeply and smile.
- Think of all the things in your life that make you happy and grateful.
- Put a label on the negative emotions you experience to make you feel like you're in control of them.
- Appreciate and love yourself more.

Just like affirmations, you can customize the fun and pleasurable activities according to your own life. The important thing is to do these activities as frequently as you can in order to help rewire your brain to focus on joy instead of negativity.

The Power of Reframing

Reframing refers to a process that first involves becoming aware of negative thinking, then making a conscious decision to substitute these thoughts for more positive and functional ones. This positive substitution is important for the stimulation of neuroplasticity in the brain.

Reframing can also be called cognitive reappraisal, specifically when it's used in cognitive behavioral therapy (CBT). This is another powerful self-development tool that you should keep practicing in order to make it a part of your life. Reframing allows you to take control of your own perspectives. Think about it this way: If you had a photo that didn't really appeal to you all that much but then someone placed it in an exquisitely lovely frame, you may look at the photo in a different way. In this example, you didn't actually touch the photo, you simple reframed it. Aou can do the same for any event or experience that happens in your life. Here are some tips:

1. If you can't change the environment, change how you relate to it.

Often, our environment plays a huge role in our experiences. This is a fact of life that we cannot change. So if you're stuck in an environment that you feel is making you hate your life but you can't get out of it, what do you do?

This is where reframing comes in. Instead of putting all of your efforts into trying to change your environment, you can try changing how you relate to it. This may not be the easiest thing to do but it's a lot better and more life-changing than stubbornly trying to change things that are beyond your control. Here are some practical ways for you to reframe your mind in order to change how you relate to your environment:

- Be realistic. The more realistic you are, the more you will come to accept your current situation.
- Try not to compare yourself to others, especially those whose situations are different from yours.
- Don't try to be someone else. Instead, try to be as genuine and authentic as you possibly can.
- Remember that empathy and generosity go a long way.
- If you think it's possible, try to change and improve the things closest to you, those that aren't beyond your control.

2. The six-step reframing process.

Another way to understand and better apply reframing is to follow these simple steps in the reframing process:

- **Step 1:** Identify what behavior or action is causing trouble.
- **Step 2:** Find out what triggers the action or behavior, and establish communication with it.
- **Step 3:** Find out if this part has a positive intent.
- **Step 4:** Access your creative resources.

- **Step 5:** Try to make a deal with this part, and commit to making it a behavior that's more resourceful.
- **Step 6:** Check to make sure that all the other parts of you are okay with the new behaviors you plan to do.

These steps engage your unconscious mind in an indirect way. So when there's something about you that you just can't place your finger on but you know that it's behind your negative or inappropriate behaviors, you can try to discover this part and "have a dialogue" with it. Obviously, this process involves a lot of self-exploration so that you can find out exactly what you need to change.

Overcoming Depression Through Neuroplasticity

When it comes to depression, there are many ways you can use neuroplasticity to help in the treatment of the condition. With the principle of repetition, using affirmations, performing activities that teach your brain to encode joy and the process of reframing, you have several options and strategies that can help you change the function and structure of your brain to help you overcome this condition.

The key is to be willing to change your brain and persist with the different strategies. As long as you do this, you can start your recovery process. Of course, it also helps to consult with professionals about this condition and use the strategies you've learned to supplement the treatment and make it more effective.

Neuroplasticity

PART 6

DEFEATING PROCRASTINATION AND OTHER ISSUES

"Whatever you want to do, do it now!
There are only so many tomorrows."

– *Michael Landon*

Neuroplasticity

CHAPTER 14

What Is Procrastination?

Procrastination is a type of habit wherein you persuade yourself to put things off for another time even though you have the time and ability to do them right now. Instead of performing important tasks, you look for trivial activities to help pass the time. All people at one time or another have experienced procrastination. If you're guilty of this, don't fret, because neuroplasticity can help with this too!

The Psychology of Procrastination

Have you ever wondered why we procrastinate? Often, people procrastinate because they overestimate the amount of time they have left to perform all their important tasks. Another reason is that people overestimate the motivation they will have in the future when there's no more time left to accomplish these tasks. For others, they underestimate the amount of time it will take them to complete certain activities. Finally, some people also procrastinate because they think that they need to be in the "proper frame of mind" to perform the task.

Aside from these, there are many other reasons why people procrastinate. No matter what your reason is, procrastination is something that you consciously have to avoid. The more you try to avoid this, the more your brain learns to accept that procrastination isn't an acceptable habit, and you should change it. When you start seeing it as a habit to break, you can start employing the strategies we discussed in Chapter 11 to break this habit and replace it with something better.

How Neuroplasticity Impacts Procrastination

There is one particular study that shows the effect of neuroplasticity on procrastination (Güntürkün, et. al., How brains of doers differ from those of procrastinators, 2018). The researchers took a unique neuroscientific approach to procrastination using fMRI brain scans. Through this study, they discovered a relationship between difficulty to initiate action and the volume of gray matter in the brain. According to the researchers, state-oriented individuals who have a higher tendency to procrastinate are those who have higher-volume amygdalas.

The reason for this may be that those who have a higher-volume amygdalas have already learned from their past experiences. Therefore, they are more extensive when it comes to the evaluation of their future actions and the possible consequences of those actions. This, in turn, causes them to hesitate, and when they do, it may result in procrastination.

So where does neuroplasticity come in?

Remember that neuroplasticity occurs when new neural pathways are created in your brain, reorganizing the structure and functions of it. Therefore, you can teach yourself new tricks through neuroplasticity. This means that even if you have a high tendency to procrastinate, you can consciously prevent this by employing the different strategies that promote neuroplasticity.

Defeating Procrastination Through Neuroplasticity

Procrastination is seldom a good thing. Often, it leads to negative consequences. So if you want to defeat this bad habit of yours, try employing these neuroplasticity-focused pointers:

- **Learn to accept reality.**

You must accept your own tendency to procrastinate. If you're in denial, you won't be able to work on this issue effectively. Have compassion for yourself so you can approach the situation in a more positive, brain-affirming way.

- **Disconnect from technology.**

Often, technological devices are the main cause of procrastination. When these gadgets are around, you can't help but pick them up and browse through blogs, social media sites and more. If this sounds familiar to you, then you should start disconnecting from these devices, especially when you know that there's work to be done.

- **Learn to prioritize.**

The more you learn how to prioritize your tasks, the more you will see how urgent they are. And when you see the importance of these tasks, you might feel more motivated to start working on them right away.

- **Focus on your tasks.**

Another reason why you might procrastinate is that you try to do too many things at once, so you feel overwhelmed. The next time you have work to do, you remember that feeling and it makes you want to do something easier or more enjoyable. If you want to avoid this, try to focus on doing your tasks one at a time. Start with the most important ones and work your way down. If you need to take a break, do it. This is a lot better than procrastinating.

- **Don't aim for perfection.**

Finally, whenever you do something, try to do your best even though it isn't perfect. When you strive too hard for perfection, this might make you feel apprehensive about the tasks you need to do. But if you loosen the reins a bit, you become more willing to perform these tasks.

CHAPTER 15

The Power of Neuroplasticity

From all the information we have discussed, you can see how powerful neuroplasticity truly is. How incredible is the fact that we can change the structure and functions of our brains in different ways in order to improve our lives? In addition to the conditions we have already discussed, you can also use neuroplasticity to help you overcome the following issues.

Defeating Addiction Through Neuroplasticity

Addiction refers to a physical and psychological inability to stop yourself from consuming a substance, drug, chemical or activity even though it causes you physical and psychological harm. Sometimes, addictions may cause a person to be unable to stop partaking in certain activities. When you suffer from an addiction, you feel like you can't control yourself.

Does this sound familiar?

Developing an addiction is a lot like forming a habit. When this happens, your brain creates a new path to support your addiction. And the more you stick with it, the stronger the path becomes. Fortunately, you can also use neuroplasticity to retrain your brain to get rid of the addiction to help yourself recover from it. Common treatment options for addictions include holistic interventions such as intensive psychotherapy. And when you pair these with neuroplasticity, you strengthen the recovery pathways that are created within your brain as a result of therapy. Then your brain starts to learn how to enjoy the process of recovery, which in turn helps improve the condition.

Defeating Phobias Through Neuroplasticity

By definition, phobias are irrational and exaggerated fears. Often, the term "phobia" refers to the fear a person feels toward a certain trigger. There are different types of phobias that may develop, and, depending on the severity, they can have a significant impact on your life.

According to research, there is a possibility that we are "biologically prepared" to fear certain things. However, we also learn phobic responses when we observe them in other people. That is why you will often see children who have phobic parents grow up into adults who have the same phobias.

This is another condition that you can apply neuroplasticity to. If you learned your phobia, this means that you have the potential to unlearn it as well. For instance, if you have a fear of heights, this doesn't mean that your brain already came wired with that fear. So you may "unlearn" your phobia through a process called "desensitization." This is where you expose yourself to what you're most fearful of which, in our example, is heights) while under controlled conditions. This exposure is coupled with different techniques that aim to help you relax in order to dampen the effect of the fear.

When you repeatedly submit to this kind of therapy, it may help you overcome your phobia. As you expose yourself to the thing you fear the most, a new path in your brain is created that tells you that you shouldn't be bothered by the thing you're afraid of. The more you expose yourself to your fear while also experiencing the relaxation techniques, the stronger this new connection becomes, until your brain gets rewired through this controlled learning technique.

Defeating Insomnia Through Neuroplasticity

This is another common condition that a lot of people all over the world suffer from. Insomnia is a sleep disorder where people aren't able to either fall asleep or stay asleep throughout the night. Unfortunately, this disrupts your body's natural healing process, which, in the long run, can have devastating effects.

When normal people sleep, there are several neuroplasticity changes that occur, and some of these are crucial to making memories stronger. If you're not able to sleep well because you're an insomniac, you may start experiencing abnormalities in your neuroplastic processes while you're awake.

In order to defeat this condition, you need to come up with a proper bedtime routine to help you fall asleep at the appropriate time. From meditation to learning how to wind down and more, there are several ways to do this. Come up with your own bedtime routine and keep practicing it every night. Although it may not work right away, we have established that the more you practice certain behaviors, the more your brain will start accepting them as part of your life. This means that, over time, your bedtime routine will become a habit that helps you fall asleep faster and stay asleep throughout the night.

Neuroplasticity and Lifestyle

Neuroplasticity is truly a wonderful thing. Although we've had this skill from the beginning, we should all feel grateful that scientists and researchers discovered the concept so that we can learn how to promote and apply neuroplasticity in our lives. Throughout this book, we have talked about different kinds of conditions and issues that you can overcome through neuroplasticity. We have also discussed several real-life tips, strategies and exercises to promote neuroplasticity as we target specific issues in our lives that we want to improve.

As a final piece of advice on the matter, if you want to promote neuroplasticity, you must also ensure that you live a healthy lifestyle. This includes:

- Exercising regularly
- Learning how to manage stress
- Balanced nutrition
- Lots of mental stimulation

Combine these with everything else you've learned in this book and you're sure to have a recipe for success!

CHAPTER 16

Binaural Beats and Brainwave Entrainment: Does It Increase Neuroplasticity?

By now you have armed yourself with enough information to help you improve your life through neuroplasticity. As a bonus, we will be talking about binaural beats and brainwave entrainment. Just like neuroplasticity, these are fairly new concepts that are just beginning to gain popularity as more and more people learn about them.

Binaural Beats and Brainwave Entrainment: Does It Increase Neuroplasticity?

But can they improve neuroplasticity? Of course! In this final chapter, we will be discussing the fundamentals of binaural beats and brainwave entrainment. You will see how they can benefit your life and your neuroplasticity journey.

What Is Brainwave Entrainment?

Throughout this book, we have learned all about neuroplasticity, its benefits and how you can use it to improve your life in different ways. Now let's look at another self-directed neuroplasticity intervention method known as brainwave entrainment. This is a fascinating concept. Ever since it came out, it has generated a lot of interest, and now a lot of people rave about because it can help reduce stress, induce sleep, facilitate your awareness, assist with mindfulness and meditation training, enhance the functioning of your brain and do so much more.

Brainwave entrainment refers to a way of producing a specific brainwave frequency. This is achieved by synchronizing your brain waves to the desired frequency using an external auditory stimulus. When you hear a rhythmic beat, your brain will start to sync its activity in order to match the beat. This is known as the "frequency following response."

Neuroplasticity

Although the technology of brain entrainment is fairly new, the concept itself has been around since music came to be. Through our history, a lot of different cultures made use of rhythmic drum beats and chanting to enter into a trance or a trance-like state. This happens because of the hypnotic quality of the rhythm, as well as the rhythm's ability to induce various states of consciousness. Basically, different kinds of beats have effects on the mood of a person. For instance, slow beats can relax or soothe you, while quick beats make you feel energized.

Our brains are continuously producing electrical activity, even when we're sleeping. Research has shown that you can actually record this electrical activity using brain waves or brainwave patterns. Then you can adjust and influence those brain waves when you stimulate them using specific types of tones and beats. This is the process we know as brainwave entrainment.

In the past, the most commonly used method of utilizing certain brainwave states was via binaural beats. Here, you would play one kind of beat in one of your ears while playing a different type of beat in your other ear. The brain automatically syncs both beats to come up with a different beat that is basically a combination of the two individual beats playing in each ear.

Binaural Beats and Brainwave Entrainment: Does It Increase Neuroplasticity?

The Different Brain Waves and Their Proposed Benefits

At the very root of your emotions, behaviors and thoughts is the communication that occurs between the different neurons of the brain. Brain waves are generated by electrical pulses from all of the neurons in your brain as they communicate with each other. Experts detect brain waves with the use of sensors that they place on a person's scalp. These brain waves are then categorized according to their bandwidths to provide a description of their functions.

To understand the concept better, you can think of your brain waves as musical notes. The brain waves that have a low frequency are like a drum beat that's deeply penetrating, while the brain waves that have a higher frequency are like a subtle flute with a high-pitched sound. Just like symphonies, these high and low frequencies connect and work with each other via harmonics.

Your brain waves keep on changing according to what you feel and do. When the dominant brain waves are the slower ones, you may start feeling dreamy, slow, tired or sluggish. On the other hand, if the dominant brain waves are the faster ones or those with higher frequencies, then you may start feeling hyper-alert or wired. Brain waves are extremely complex and reflect varying aspects when they happen in the different parts of your brain. The unit of measurement of brainwave speed is Hertz or cycles per second, and each of the brainwave frequencies has its own benefits. Let's take a look at these now:

- **Delta waves (from 0.5 to 3.0 Hz)**

These are the slowest brain waves, but they are also the loudest. Delta waves have a low frequency, and they're deeply penetrating. These waves are produced when you have a deep and dreamless sleep, or when you're practicing deep meditation. They suspend your external awareness. Regeneration and healing are activated when your brain produces delta waves. This is why deep sleep is important for the restorative healing process. The benefits of this brainwave frequency include:

  - Deep sleep that promotes natural healing, as well as the health of the immune system.

  - When you're in this state, your body releases anti-aging hormones such as DHEA and melatonin.

  - Also, the level of human growth hormone (HGH) increases because the pituitary gland is stimulated. HGH is important because it maintains the health of the joints, cartilage, skin and bone density. It can also help alleviate physical pain.

Binaural Beats and Brainwave Entrainment: Does It Increase Neuroplasticity?

If you have too few of these brain waves, this causes poor sleep and an inability to rejuvenate the body and revitalize the brain. Conversely, if you have too much of these brain waves, this may lead to learning problems, severe ADHD, brain injuries and an inability to think.

- **Theta waves (from 3.0 to 8.0 Hz)**

These brain waves occur when we sleep, and they're also dominant when you meditate deeply. Theta waves are your gateway to intuition, memory and learning. In theta, your senses are hidden from the outside world. Instead, you focus on the signals coming from within.

This is considered a "twilight state" that you are only able to fleetingly experience when you drift off to sleep or when you wake up. In theta, you're beyond your conscious awareness. You're in a dream with your intuition and vivid imagery. This is where you hold your nightmares, fears and troubled history. Some of the benefits of this brainwave frequency are:

   o   An increase in relaxation, emotional connection, intuition and creativity.

   o   It promotes a more restful sleep, thereby helping improve your physical healing.

- Beneficial hormones that are associated with longevity and health are released.
- There is a reduction in stress, anxiety and mental fatigue.

If you have too few of these brain waves, this causes stress, anxiety and poor emotional awareness. Conversely, if you have too much of these brain waves, this may lead to depression, inattentiveness, ADHD, hyperactivity and impulsivity.

- **Alpha waves (from 8.0 to 12.0 Hz)**

These brain waves happen when our thoughts are flowing quietly, but not necessarily during meditation. Alpha brain waves promote "the power of now," which is when you fully experience every present moment. It's the brain's resting state, and it helps in the brain's overall learning, calmness, mental coordination, alertness and mind-body integration. Here are some benefits of these brain waves:

- You feel more relaxed, your levels of anxiety are reduced and it also eases the effects of depression and stress.
- It helps reduce the levels of blood pressure, along with chronic pain.

Binaural Beats and Brainwave Entrainment: Does It Increase Neuroplasticity?

- It increases happiness, energy, motivation, athletic performance and cerebral blood flow.

If you have too few of these brain waves, this causes OCD, high stress, anxiety and insomnia. Conversely, if you have too much of these brain waves, this may lead to an inability to focus, daydreaming and becoming too relaxed.

- **Beta waves (from 12.0 to 38.0 Hz)**

These brain waves occur when we are in our normal state of consciousness when we're awake. They dominate whenever we direct our attention to the outside world and perform cognitive tasks. These brain waves promote "fast activity," making us attentive, alert and fully focused on mental activity, problem-solving, decision-making and judgments.

This brainwave frequency can be divided further into three different bands, namely hi-beta (which involves excitement, thoughts that are highly complex, the integration of new experiences and high levels of anxiety); beta (which involves high engagement and actively trying to figure things out); and lo-beta (which involves musing or "fast idle"). The benefits of beta waves include:

- Being able to focus consciously, solving problems effectively and having improved memory.

- This is when the fight-or-flight response activates, which is crucial in dangerous situations.
  - Improvement in alertness, reasoning, logic, concentration and critical thinking.

If you have too few of these brain waves, this causes ADHD, depression, daydreaming and poor cognition. Conversely, if you have too much of these brain waves, this may lead to anxiety, an inability to relax, too much adrenaline, high arousal and stress.

- **Gamma waves (from 38.0 to 42.0 Hz)**

These brain waves are the fastest ones, and they're associated with simultaneous information processing from the different parts of the brain. Gamma brain waves transmit information in a quiet but quick way. They're the most subtle brain waves, so you need to quiet your mind if you want to access them.

In the past, researchers dismissed gamma brain waves as "spare brain noise." That is, until they found out that these waves were highly active in people who were in states of altruism, universal love and other "higher virtues." These brain waves also occur above the neuronal firing frequency, so experts aren't really sure how they are generated. According to speculation, the rhythms of gamma brain waves modulate consciousness and perception. Here are the benefits of gamma brain waves:

- o They improve information processing, REM sleep, perception, learning, cognition and the senses.
- o Being compassionate and having a higher intelligence level.
- o Being able to control one's self more effectively.
- o Increased awareness through the senses and experiencing natural happiness more.

If you have too few of these brain waves, this causes ADHD, learning disabilities and depression. Conversely, if you have too much of these brain waves, this may lead to anxiety, stress and high arousal.

You cannot separate your daily experiences from your brainwave profile. When your brain waves aren't in perfect balance, you will start experiencing problems in your neuro-physical or emotional health.

Evidence Showing How Binaural Beats or Brainwave Entrainment Help Neuroplasticity

A good amount of research has been done about binaural beats and brainwave entrainment, and how they help neuroplasticity. For instance, in one study, researchers found that when a person listens to binaural beats for a certain amount of time, there is a change in their arousal levels (Padmanabhan, Hildreth & Laws, A prospective, randomised, controlled study examining binaural beat audio and preoperative anxiety in patients undergoing general anaesthesia for day case surgery, 2005). They believe that binaural beats stimulate specific systems of the brain, which causes these changes.

In another small study, the results showed that the use of binaural beats in the alpha, delta and theta patterns cause a positive impact on the body (Giampapa, Binaural Beats Therapy Stimulates Long Life & Wellbeing Hormones, n.d.). These beats promote the production of DHEA, cortisol and melatonin, three types of hormones.

The use of binaural beats can also promote a decrease in insulin-like growth factor, dopamine and anxiety, as shown by a study conducted in Oregon's National College of Natural Medicine (Wahbeh, Calabrese & Zwickey, Binaural beat technology in humans: a pilot study to assess psychologic and physiologic effects, 2007). The participants of this study also experienced an improvement in their quality of life. The researchers concluded that binaural beats may help in the improvement of self-reported anxiety.

Binaural Beats and Brainwave Entrainment: Does It Increase Neuroplasticity?

All of these studies and more show how binaural beats can help cause changes in the brain. Since brainwave entrainment works with basically the same core principle as binaural beats, the results of these studies may also apply. Of course, more studies are being conducted, and are needed to provide more evidence on how binaural beats or brainwave entrainment may help with neuroplasticity. One thing's for sure: They are highly effective, which is why more and more people are starting to get interested in them.

The Benefits of Brainwave Entrainment or Binaural Beats

As we have already learned, brainwave entrainment and binaural beats are powerful methods of utilizing sounds to alter the state of the brain. Since the brain operates at various wavelengths, you can make adjustments to them depending on what aspect you want to improve. Take a look at these benefits:

- **Increased creativity**

This comes from beta waves. When you awaken up from a deep sleep or when you try to break through the lull you feel every afternoon, beta brain waves can help increase your creativity and bring you into a heightened state of alertness.

- **Stress relief**

This comes from alpha waves. When you find your mind racing at the end of the day because you experienced a lot of stress, alpha brain waves can help generate a state of relaxation by calming your mind.

- **Improved learning**

This comes from theta waves. When you want to learn new things, the ideal frequency is theta. However, you can't really learn while you're asleep! So you can use brain entrainment to tune in your brain to the theta state while you're awake to improve your memory and learning.

- **Rejuvenating rest**

This comes from delta waves. When you use these waves, you can fall asleep more easily, and they can even improve your sleep quality. Then, when you wake up, you feel a lot more rested.

- **Anxiety reduction**

One of the more popular programs of brainwave entrainment is known as "holosync," since it's highly effective for the reduction of anxiety. Through this, you can suppress your negative thoughts and open your mind to more positive thinking.

Binaural Beats and Brainwave Entrainment: Does It Increase Neuroplasticity?

- **Pressure relief**

Brainwave entrainment can also help relieve pressure, especially when you use it to induce brain waves to move into the alpha state rather than the beta state. This, in turn, reduces the source of pressure that come from beta waves.

- **Improved ingenuity**

You can also use brainwave entrainment to excite your brain waves from beta states (where intellectual reasoning occurs) to alpha states (which help improve visualization and ingenuity).

- **Easier meditation**

You will also find it easier to meditate when you use brainwave entrainment. This helps induce the required brain waves so that you can achieve a meditative state more easily.

Apart from these benefits, there are also a lot of testimonials from those who have actually used binaural beats and brainwave entrainment. If you need more convincing, here are some excerpts from the statements of real-life people: [1]

---

[1] Testimonials retrieved from
https://www.activemindsglobal.com/testimonials1/

- "Today is the 35th day I have used the program. I am thrilled to say it has genuinely made a tangible difference in my ability to remember information, deal with the stress of work and crucially unwind and relax as soon as I leave the office." - Nick Lyus

- "Now, after two months of using your programs, I not only ha very clear thought processes, but I also have and retain my memories back to when I was a small child. - Ross Joyner

- "After using it for all these days, I feel more energetic, more calmer like never before, increased concentration and getting good grades in my college!" - Prasannaa

- "Without a doubt, when I have been listening to the recordings I am more focused, energized and "in the moment" – I love it! And I've also found it's a damn good hangover cure!" - Matt Court, product manager, NZ

Finding the Best Resources

As you can see, binaural beats and brainwave entrainment are highly beneficial. If you're just like me and want to improve your life through neuroplasticity, these can definitely help you out. There are plenty of resources available for these programs, but I personally believe that the ones below are the best. I have used these resources myself, and have experienced all of the benefits, which helped me move forward as my condition improved.

Click on the image below so I can add you to my email list. Then you can start your healing journey along with me and the many others who have started applying neuroplasticity to their lives. Let's all work together to lead better lives!

http://bit.ly/BinauralBeatsCollection

Neuroplasticity

Bibliography

4 Benefits of Brainwave Entrainment. (2019). Retrieved from https://www.mindmovies.com/blogroll/4-benefits-of-brainwave-entrainment

5 Brain Exercises to Foster Flexible Thinking. (2019). Retrieved from https://www.gaiam.com/blogs/discover/5-brain-exercises-to-foster-flexible-thinking

5 Types Of Brain Waves Frequencies: Gamma, Beta, Alpha, Theta, Delta. (2019). Retrieved from https://mentalhealthdaily.com/2014/04/15/5-types-of-brain-waves-frequencies-gamma-beta-alpha-theta-delta/

7 Ways To Create More Joy In Your Life. (2019). Retrieved from https://www.mindbodygreen.com/0-10143/7-ways-to-create-more-joy-in-your-life.html

7 Ways To Increase Your Cognitive Flexibility. (2019). Retrieved from https://mentalhealthdaily.com/2015/07/26/7-ways-to-increase-your-cognitive-flexibility/

10 Ways to Make Yourself Happier in 30 Seconds or Less. (2019). Retrieved from https://www.psychologytoday.com/us/blog/changepower/201607/10-ways-make-yourself-happier-in-30-seconds-or-less

11 Powerful Affirmations to Help Treat Depression and Anxiety. (2019). Retrieved from https://www.powerofpositivity.com/11-powerful-affirmations-help-treat-depression-anxiety/

A prospective, randomised, controlled study examining binaural beat audio and pre-operative anxiety in patients undergoing general anaesthesia for day case surgery. (2019). Retrieved from https://onlinelibrary.wiley.com/doi/full/10.1111/j.1365-2044.2005.04287.x

Adult Neurogenesis | About memory. (2019). Retrieved from https://www.memory-key.com/memory/neurogenesis

Bibliography

Alsaleh, M., & Kubitary, A. Treatment by repeating phrases of positive thoughts (TRPPT): A new effective treatment tool against psychological troubles (PSYT) (Depression, anxiety, stress, low self-esteem and dissatisfaction in life) in multiple sclerosis patients and students, a controlled and randomized pilot study. (2019). Retrieved from http://www.alliedacademies.org/articles/treatment-by-repeating-phrases-of-positive-thoughts-trppt-a-new-effective-treatment-tool-against-psychological-troubles-psyt-depre-6075.html

Anderson, M., & Finlay, B. (2019). Allocating structure to function: the strong links between neuroplasticity and natural selection. Retrieved from https://www.frontiersin.org/articles/10.3389/fnhum.2013.00918/full

A novel primary culture method for high-purity satellite glial cells derived from rat dorsal root ganglion. (2019). Retrieved from http://www.nrronline.org/article.asp?issn=1673-5374;year=2019;volume=14;issue=2;spage=339;epage=345;aulast=Wang

Baum, I. How Your Body Can React To Chronic Isolation. (2019). Retrieved from https://www.bustle.com/articles/196816-11-things-that-can-happen-to-your-mind-body-if-you-dont-socialize-for-a

Benefits of Brainwave Entrainment. (2019). Retrieved from https://www.levelupculture.com/blogs/articles/benefits-of-brainwave-entrainment

Better Than Before: Powerful Neuroplasticity Principles To Rewire The Brain & Break Negative Habits. (2019). Retrieved from https://www.huffpost.com/entry/better-than-before-powerful-neuroplasticity-principles_b_58bf0a9ce4b04d49eb262a70

Beyond the neuron: Emerging roles of glial cells in neuroscience | PLOS ECR Community. (2019). Retrieved from https://blogs.plos.org/thestudentblog/2016/01/25/glial cells/

Brain Cells. (2019). Retrieved from https://www.enchantedlearning.com/subjects/anatomy/brain/Neuron.shtml

Brain cells | The Brain Tumour Charity. (2019). Retrieved from https://www.thebraintumourcharity.org/brain-tumour-diagnosis-treatment/how-brain-tumours-are-diagnosed/brain-tumour-biology/brain-cells/

Brain Health With Binaural Beats. (2019). Retrieved from https://www.healthline.com/health-news/your-brain-on-binaural-beats#8

Bibliography

Brain plasticity and motor practice in cognitive aging. (2019). Retrieved from https://www.frontiersin.org/articles/10.3389/fnagi.2014.00031/full

BrainHQ from Posit Science. (2019). Retrieved from https://www.brainhq.com/?v4=true&fr=y

Brain, Heal Thyself - How Neuroplasticity Hurts and Heals - Extraordinary Brain. (2019). Retrieved from http://www.extraordinarybrain.com/brain-heal-thyself-neuroplasticity/

Breaking Bad Habits, With Neuroplasticity. (2019). Retrieved from https://www.eduguide.org/content/2015/02/13/breaking-bad-habits-with-neuroplasticity/

Bremner, J. (2019). Traumatic stress: effects on the brain. Retrieved from https://www.ncbi.nlm.nih.gov/pmc/articles/PMC3181836/

Brownson, T. The Incredible Power of Reframing - A Daring Adventure. (2019). Retrieved from https://www.adaringadventure.com/power-of-reframing/

Bubnis, D. (2019). Binaural beats therapy: Benefits and how they work. Retrieved from https://www.medicalnewstoday.com/articles/320019.php

Building Students' Cognitive Flexibility. (2019). Retrieved from https://www.edutopia.org/blog/building-students-cognitive-flexibility-judy-willis

Canino, Frank J. Learned-Helplessness Theory: Implications for Research in Learning Disabilities 1981. (2019). Retrieved from https://journals.sagepub.com/doi/10.1177/002246698101500408

Cognitive flexibility. (2019). Retrieved from https://en.wikipedia.org/wiki/Cognitive_flexibility

Cohen, J. 19 Ways to "Grow" Your Brain (& New Hope for Brain Injury) - SelfHacked. (2019). Retrieved from https://selfhacked.com/blog/can-regrow-brain/

Correlation Between Structures of the Brain Function and PTSD. (2019). Retrieved from https://www.verywellmind.com/what-exactly-does-ptsd-do-to-the-brain-2797210

Deiss, R. Lead Magnets | 9 Lead Magnet Ideas with Examples. (2019). Retrieved from https://www.digitalmarketer.com/blog/lead-magnet-ideas-funnel/

Depression: Effects on the Brain. (2019). Retrieved from https://www.healthline.com/health/depression/effects-brain#3

Bibliography

Difference between Neuroplasticity and Neurogenesis - 9zest. (2019). Retrieved from https://9zest.com/guide/difference-neurogenesis-neuroplasticity/

Different Types Of Brain Waves And Their Benefits. (2019). Retrieved from https://www.curejoy.com/content/different-types-brain-waves/

Do Exercises Aimed at Increasing Neuroplasticity Work?. (2019). Retrieved from https://www.huffpost.com/entry/do-exercises-aimed-at-inc_n_13023114

Effect of Environmental Enrichment on Stress Related Systems in Rats. (2019). Retrieved from https://onlinelibrary.wiley.com/doi/abs/10.1111/j.1365-2826.2004.01173.x

Environmental enrichment. (2019). Retrieved from https://en.wikipedia.org/wiki/Environmental_enrichment

Environmental Enrichment and Neuronal Plasticity. (2019). Retrieved from http://www.oxfordhandbooks.com/view/10.1093/oxfordhb/9780190635374.001.0001/oxfordhb-9780190635374-e-13

Environmental enrichment promotes neural plasticity and cognitive ability in fish | Proceedings of the Royal

Society B: Biological Sciences. (2019). Retrieved from https://royalsocietypublishing.org/doi/full/10.1098/rspb.2013.1331

Environmental Factors Promoting Neural Plasticity: Insights from Animal and Human Studies. (2019). Retrieved from https://www.hindawi.com/journals/np/2017/7219461/

Environmental Factors Promoting Neural Plasticity: Insights from Animal and Human Studies. (2019). Retrieved from https://www.ncbi.nlm.nih.gov/pmc/articles/PMC5504954/

Erickson, R. (2019). Neuroplasticity and Trauma: Can Brain Science Give Us a New Perspective on Healing? - NICABM. Retrieved from https://www.nicabm.com/brain-neuroplasticity-and-trauma-can-brain-science-give-us-a-new-perspective-on-healing-2/

Exercise Promotes Neuroplasticity in Both Healthy and Depressed Brains: An fMRI Pilot Study. (2019). Retrieved from https://www.ncbi.nlm.nih.gov/pmc/articles/PMC5554572/

Bibliography

Explainer: nature, nurture and neuroplasticity. (2019). Retrieved from https://theconversation.com/explainer-nature-nurture-and-neuroplasticity-10734

Find an EMDR Therapist | Psychologist | Counselor | Coach for EMDR. (2019). Retrieved from https://www.emdrtherapistnetwork.com/find-an-emdr-therapist.html

francis, o., iran, z., Alban, D., Alban, D., Assad, M., & Alban, D. et al. 15 Brain Exercises to Keep Your Mind Sharp. (2019). Retrieved from https://bebrainfit.com/brain-exercises/

Franco, F. Learned Helplessness and C-PTSD. (2019). Retrieved from https://psychcentral.com/lib/learned-helplessness-and-c-ptsd/

Gilani, N. Six Types of Neuroglia (2019). Retrieved from https://sciencing.com/six-types-neuroglia-6302092.html

Hamilton, et. al. Alexia for Braille following bilateral occipitalstroke in an early blind woman (2019). Retrieved from https://pdfs.semanticscholar.org/c93b/a3bbc7ee9d42b80cb1e6b312ca608c249839.pdf

Handel, S. (2019). Identify Your Habit Loops: The Basic Structure Behind Every Single Habit. Retrieved from https://www.theemotionmachine.com/habit-loops/

Hanscom, D. Changing Your Story – Reframing. (2019). Retrieved from https://backincontrol.com/changing-your-story-reframing/

Helpful Repetitive Thinking in Depression. (2019). Retrieved from https://www.psychologytoday.com/us/blog/mood-thought/201307/helpful-repetitive-thinking-in-depression

Hess, G. What is Neuroplasticity and How Does It Affect Us? | Consensus. (2019). Retrieved from https://www.goconsensus.com/blog/what-is-neuroplasticity-and-how-does-it-affect-us/

How Do Neuroplasticity and Neurogenesis Rewire Your Brain?. (2019). Retrieved from https://www.psychologytoday.com/intl/blog/the-athletes-way/201702/how-do-neuroplasticity-and-neurogenesis-rewire-your-brain

How Neuroplasticity Can Help You Get Rid Of Your Bad Habits. (2019). Retrieved from https://www.huffingtonpost.com.au/2017/11/20/how-neuroplasticity-can-help-you-get-rid-of-your-bad-habits_a_23283591/

How the Brain Changes When You Meditate - Mindful. (2019). Retrieved from https://www.mindful.org/how-the-brain-changes-when-you-meditate/

Bibliography

How to Break Bad Habits - Understanding the 'Habit Loop'. (2019). Retrieved from https://blog.thefabulous.co/how-habits-work-making-and-breaking-habits-with-the-habit-loop/

How to Change Your Behavior? The Science behind Neuroplasticity – Kwik Learning. (2019). Retrieved from https://kwiklearning.com/kwik-tips/how-to-change-your-behavior-the-science-behind-neuroplasticity/

How to Improve Cognitive Flexibility? | Toru. (2019). Retrieved from http://toruinstitute.com/how-to-improve-cognitive-flexibility/

How to Increase Neuroplasticity (Improve Your Intelligence and Brain Flexibility) - Siim Land. (2019). Retrieved from https://siimland.com/how-to-increase-neuroplasticity/

How You Can Train Your Brain to Create New Habits. (2019). Retrieved from https://examinedexistence.com/how-you-can-train-your-brain-to-create-new-habits/

http://time.com. (2019). Retrieved from http://time.com/4856925/be-happy-more-joy/

Hunter, W. (2019). 29 Ways to Increase Neurogenesis - SelfHacked. Retrieved from https://selfhacked.com/blog/ways-increase-neurogenesis/

If You Want To Change The World, First Change Yourself: Four Steps To Making A Positive Impact. (2019). Retrieved from https://hackernoon.com/if-you-want-to-change-the-world-first-change-yourself-four-steps-to-making-a-positive-impact-644aacc97be7

Increased Use-Dependent Plasticity in Chronic Insomnia. (2019). Retrieved from https://www.ncbi.nlm.nih.gov/pmc/articles/PMC3920319/

Jabr, F. Know Your Neurons: How to Classify Different Types of Neurons in the Brain's Forest. (2019). Retrieved from https://blogs.scientificamerican.com/brainwaves/know-your-neurons-classifying-the-many-types-of-cells-in-the-neuron-forest/

Jackson, F. (2019). Benefits of brainwave entrainment. Retrieved from https://www.paranetinfo.com/benefits-of-brainwave-entrainment/

Jon Lieff, M.D., How Does Neuroplasticity Work? (2019). Retrieved from http://jonlieffmd.com/blog/how-does-neuroplasticity-work

Kelly, D. Brain Plasticity and the Power of Affirmations. (2019). Retrieved from http://yogachicago.com/2014/11/brain-plasticity-and-the-power-of-affirmations/

Bibliography

Kolassa, I., Elbert, T., Structural and Functional Neuroplasticity in Relation to Traumatic Stress 2007. (2019). Retrieved from https://journals.sagepub.com/doi/abs/10.1111/j.1467-8721.2007.00529.x?journalCode=cdpa

Language learning boosts brain plasticity and ability to code new information. (2019). Retrieved from https://www.medicalnewstoday.com/articles/312708.php

Learning, memory and brain plasticity in posttraumatic stress disorder: context matters. - PubMed - NCBI. (2019). Retrieved from https://www.ncbi.nlm.nih.gov/pubmed/23945193

Legg, T. Phobias: Symptoms, types, causes, and treatment. (2019). Retrieved from https://www.medicalnewstoday.com/articles/249347.php

Lifestyle Modulators of Neuroplasticity: How Physical Activity, Mental Engagement, and Diet Promote Cognitive Health during Aging. (2019). Retrieved from https://www.hindawi.com/journals/np/2017/3589271/

Make the brain a joyful place and combat depression. (2019). Retrieved from https://labblog.uofmhealth.org/lab-report/make-brain-a-joyful-place-and-combat-depression

Massive cortical reorganization in sighted Braille readers. (2019). Retrieved from https://elifesciences.org/articles/10762

Mateus-Pinheiro, Patricio, Bessa, Sousa, & Pinto. Cell genesis and dendritic plasticity: a neuroplastic pas de deux in the onset and remission from depression. (2019). Retrieved from https://www.ncbi.nlm.nih.gov/pmc/articles/PMC3690420/

Mindfulness-based treatments for posttraumatic stress disorder: a review of the treatment literature and neurobiological evidence. (2019). Retrieved from https://www.ncbi.nlm.nih.gov/pmc/articles/PMC5747539/

Morelli, K. EMDR, PTSD, Neuroplasticity and "Limbic System Therapy". (2019). Retrieved from https://birthtouch.com/2017/10/emdr-neuroplasticity-and-limbic-system-therapy/

Murrell, D. (2019). Insomnia: Causes, symptoms, and treatments. Retrieved from https://www.medicalnewstoday.com/articles/9155.php

Myelin Facilitation of Whole Brain Neuroplasticity. (2019). Retrieved from http://jonlieffmd.com/blog/myelin-facilitation-of-whole-brain-neuroplasticity

Bibliography

Myelination - an overview | ScienceDirect Topics. (2019). Retrieved from https://www.sciencedirect.com/topics/medicine-and-dentistry/myelination

Myelination at a glance. (2019). Retrieved from http://jcs.biologists.org/content/127/14/2999

NCBI. (2019). Retrieved from https://www.ncbi.nlm.nih.gov/pmc/articles/PMC5649212/

Neural activity promotes brain plasticity through myelin growth, researchers find. (2019). Retrieved from https://med.stanford.edu/news/all-news/2014/04/neural-activity-promotes-brain-plasticity-through-myelin-growth-study-finds.html

Neural Plasticity Is Involved in Physiological Sleep, Depressive Sleep Disturbances, and Antidepressant Treatments. (2019). Retrieved from https://www.ncbi.nlm.nih.gov/pmc/articles/PMC5664320/

Neural Reorganization Following Sensory Loss: The Opportunity Of Change. (2019). Retrieved from https://www.ncbi.nlm.nih.gov/pmc/articles/PMC3898172/

Neuroplasticity 101 - Holistic Health Masterclass. (2019). Retrieved from http://www.holistic-health-masterclass.com/neuroplasticity-the-10-fundamentals-of-rewiring-your-brain/

Neuroplasticity: An Extraordinary Discovery of the Twentieth Century. (2019). Retrieved from https://www.edubloxtutor.com/neuroplasticity/

Neuroplasticity - an overview | ScienceDirect Topics. (2019). Retrieved from https://www.sciencedirect.com/topics/agricultural-and-biological-sciences/neuroplasticity

Neuroplasticity and Addiction Recovery. (2019). Retrieved from https://www.psychologytoday.com/us/blog/ending-addiction-good/201302/neuroplasticity-and-addiction-recovery

Neuroplasticity and Depression. (2019). Retrieved from https://www.psychologytoday.com/intl/blog/heal-your-brain/201107/neuroplasticity-and-depression

Neuroplasticity and Healthy Lifestyle: How Can We Understand This Relationship?. (2019). Retrieved from https://www.ncbi.nlm.nih.gov/pmc/articles/PMC5662798/

Neuroplasticity and Motor Rehabilitation in Multiple Sclerosis. (2019). Retrieved from https://www.ncbi.nlm.nih.gov/pmc/articles/PMC4364082/

Bibliography

Neuroplasticity and Myelin: Fascinating Brain Mysteries |Education & Teacher Conferences. (2019). Retrieved from https://www.learningandthebrain.com/blog/neuroplasticity-and-myelin/

NEUROPLASTICITY AND REWIRING THE BRAIN – Healing Trauma Center. (2019). Retrieved from https://healingtraumacenter.com/neuroplasticity-and-rewiring-the-brain/

Neuroplasticity: Brainwave Entrainment — Steemit. (2019). Retrieved from https://steemit.com/steemiteducation/@cabbagepatch/neuroplasticity-brainwave-entrainment

neuroplasticity-cognitive-exercises.pdf. (2019). Retrieved from https://drive.google.com/file/d/1rXFOYaL3MoWveH3aOf7N8bFmF1xijXhd/view

Neuroplasticity Exercises – Brain Workouts to Enhance Performance. (2019). Retrieved from https://blog.udemy.com/neuroplasticity-exercises/

Neuroplasticity in addictive disorders. (2019). Retrieved from https://www.ncbi.nlm.nih.gov/pmc/articles/PMC3181920/

Neuroplasticity in old age: Sustained fivefold induction of hippocampal neurogenesis by long-term environmental enrichment. (2019). Retrieved from https://onlinelibrary.wiley.com/doi/abs/10.1002/ana.10262

Neuroplasticity in response to cognitive behavior therapy for social anxiety disorder. (2019). Retrieved from https://www.nature.com/articles/tp2015218

Neuroplasticity in stroke recovery. The role of microglia in engaging and modifying synapses and networks. (2019). Retrieved from https://onlinelibrary.wiley.com/doi/abs/10.1111/ejn.13959

neuroplasticity-sensorial-motoric-exercises.pdf. (2019). Retrieved from https://drive.google.com/file/d/1irFsfsIyjKGMPrZH6JoQzFM-Rpnl-Az9/view

neuroplasticity-social-exercises.pdf. (2019). Retrieved from https://drive.google.com/file/d/1uBnPjV5i6s62vPhHI9wpdjHALy46_CB-/view

Neuroplasticity Studies Reveal Your Brain's Amazing Malleability. (2019). Retrieved from https://articles.mercola.com/sites/articles/archive/2015/01/15/neuroplasticity-brain-health.aspx

Neuroplasticity subserving motor skill learning. (2019). Retrieved from

Bibliography

https://www.ncbi.nlm.nih.gov/pmc/articles/PMC3217208/

Neuroplasticity: the potential for lifelong brain development. (2019). Retrieved from https://sharpbrains.com/resources/1-brain-fitness-fundamentals/neuroplasticity-the-potential-for-lifelong-brain-development/

Neuroplasticity: The Truth in PTSD Recovery - Ticlearn. (2019). Retrieved from http://psychink.com/ticlearn/blog/2014/06/12/neuroplasticity-truth-ptsd-recovery/

Neuroplasticity: What You Need to Know in PTSD Recovery | HealthyPlace. (2019). Retrieved from https://www.healthyplace.com/blogs/traumaptsdblog/2013/03/neuroplasticity-what-you-need-to-know-in-ptsd-recovery

Neuroplasticity: Your Brain's Amazing Ability to Form New Habits | Refocuser. (2019). Retrieved from http://www.refocuser.com/2009/05/neuroplasticity-your-brains-amazing-ability-to-form-new-habits/

NLP Techniques: Six-Step Reframing | Grass Roots NLP. (2019). Retrieved from https://grassrootsnlp.com/nlp-techniques-six-step-reframing

Oscar Ybarra, Eugene Burnstein, Piotr Winkielman, Matthew C. Keller, Melvin Manis, Emily Chan, Joel Rodriguez. Mental Exercising Through Simple

Socializing: Social Interaction Promotes General Cognitive Functioning, 2008. (2019). Retrieved from https://journals.sagepub.com/doi/10.1177/0146167207310454

Overcoming Destructive Habits with Neuroplasticity | Balanced Achievement. (2019). Retrieved from https://balancedachievement.com/psychology/neuroplasticity/

PET scan of the brain for depression. (2019). Retrieved from https://www.mayoclinic.org/tests-procedures/pet-scan/multimedia/-pet-scan-of-the-brain-for-depression/img-20007400

Physical Exercise Enhances Neuroplasticity and Delays Alzheimer's Disease. (2019). Retrieved from https://www.ncbi.nlm.nih.gov/pmc/articles/PMC6296269/

Picking an EMDR Therapist? - EMDR Consulting. (2019). Retrieved from https://www.emdrconsulting.com/picking-an-emdr-therapist/

Poor social skills may be harmful to health. (2019). Retrieved from https://www.sciencedaily.com/releases/2017/11/171106090116.htm

Post-traumatic stress disorder (PTSD) - Symptoms and causes. (2019). Retrieved from https://www.mayoclinic.org/diseases-conditions/post-traumatic-stress-disorder/symptoms-causes/syc-20355967

Predegenerated Schwann cells–a novel prospect for cell therapy for glaucoma: neuroprotection, neuroregeneration and neuroplasticity. (2019). Retrieved from https://www.nature.com/articles/srep23187

Ravenscraft, E. Focus On Intrinsic Motivation to More Effectively Build New Habits. (2019). Retrieved from https://lifehacker.com/focus-on-intrinsic-motivation-to-more-effectively-build-1791603993

Rewire your brain to beat procrastination. (2019). Retrieved from https://medium.com/taking-note/rewire-your-brain-to-beat-procrastination-30b7d172c9d2

Rewiring the Brain to Eliminate Fear. (2019). Retrieved from https://www.psychologytoday.com/us/blog/demystifying-psychiatry/201311/rewiring-the-brain-eliminate-fear

Reyes, Z. The Roles Neuroplasticity and EMDR Play in Healing from Childhood Trauma. (2019). Retrieved from https://psychcentral.com/lib/the-roles-neuroplasticity-and-emdr-play-in-healing-from-childhood-trauma/

Saripalli, V. Addiction: Definition, symptoms, withdrawal, and treatment. (2019). Retrieved from https://www.medicalnewstoday.com/articles/323465.php

Schwartz, A. Shame in Complex PTSD. (2019). Retrieved from https://drarielleschwartz.com/shame-in-complex-ptsd-dr-arielle-schwartz/#.XMW6EP5S_IV

Sensory Deprivation and Brain Plasticity. (2019). Retrieved from https://www.hindawi.com/journals/np/si/191938/cfp/

Shiel Jr., W. Definition of Neuroplasticity. (2019). Retrieved from https://www.medicinenet.com/script/main/art.asp?articlekey=40362

Sign language 'heard' in the auditory cortex. (2019). Retrieved from https://www.nature.com/articles/16376

Simple Pleasures. (2019). Retrieved from https://www.apa.org/science/about/psa/2004/11/berridge

Smith, G. (2019). Aging and neuroplasticity. Retrieved from https://www.ncbi.nlm.nih.gov/pmc/articles/PMC3622467/

Bibliography

Sovtexas., New study finds physical differences in depressed brains (2019). Retrieved from https://www.sovtexas.com/treatment/new-study-finds-physical-differences-depressed-brains/

Study reveals what depression, anxiety look like in the brain. (2019). Retrieved from https://www.medicalnewstoday.com/articles/320112.php

Testimonials | Best Brainwave Entrainment | Active Minds Global | NeuroLearn+® | WorkSharp® | RevitaMind®. (2019). Retrieved from https://www.activemindsglobal.com/testimonials1/

The 4 Ways Depression Can Physically Affect Your Brain. (2019). Retrieved from https://www.healthline.com/health/depression-physical-effects-on-the-brain#1

The 7 Most Effective Ways to Rewire Your Brain with Affirmations | Brain Sync | Brain Sync. (2019). Retrieved from http://www.brainsync.com/blog/rewire-your-brain-with-affirmations/

The Effect of Sensory Deprivation on Neuroplasticity Neuroplasticity: refers to the brain's ability to rearrange the connection between its neurons – that. - ppt download. (2019). Retrieved from https://slideplayer.com/slide/9364555/

The Importance of Socialization for Brain Development. (2019). Retrieved from https://exploringyourmind.com/socialization-brain-development/

The Neural Signature of Procrastination. (2019). Retrieved from https://www.psychologytoday.com/intl/blog/dont-delay/201808/the-neural-signature-procrastination

The Power of Neuroplasticity | MyBrainWare. (2019). Retrieved from https://mybrainware.com/knowledge-center/blogs/the-power-of-neuroplasticity/

The Psychology Behind Why We Wait Until the Last Minute to Do Things. (2019). Retrieved from https://www.verywellmind.com/the-psychology-of-procrastination-2795944

The PTSD Solution: New Hope through Brain Plasticity. (2019). Retrieved from https://www.psychologytoday.com/us/blog/redefining-stress/200902/the-ptsd-solution-new-hope-through-brain-plasticity

The Neuroscience of Phobias. (2019). Retrieved from https://christopher-delaney.com/2014/06/11/the-neuroscience-of-phobias/

The Role of Neural Plasticity in Depression: From Hippocampus to Prefrontal Cortex. (2019). Retrieved from https://www.hindawi.com/journals/np/2017/6871089/

The Science Behind Adopting New Habits (And Making Them Stick). (2019). Retrieved from https://www.forbes.com/sites/quora/2018/02/13/the-science-behind-adopting-new-habits-and-making-them-stick/#79bbf63b43c7

The Science Of Habit Formation And Change. (2019). Retrieved from https://fs.blog/2012/03/everything-you-need-to-know-about-habits-the-science-of-habit-formation-and-change/

The Science of Trauma, Mindfulness, and PTSD - Mindful. (2019). Retrieved from https://www.mindful.org/the-science-of-trauma-mindfulness-ptsd/

The Unexpected Drawbacks To Positive Thinking. (2019). Retrieved from https://www.fastcompany.com/3067650/the-unexpected-drawbacks-to-positive-thinking

The Very Intelligent Choroid Plexus Epithelial Cell. (2019). Retrieved from http://jonlieffmd.com/blog/the-very-intelligent-choroid-plexus-epithelial-cell

This Is The Only Type Of Brain Training That Works, According To Science. (2019). Retrieved from https://www.fastcompany.com/40451692/this-is-the-only-type-of-brain-training-that-works-according-to-science

Train the Brain! Motor Learning Strategies to Promote Neural Plasticity in Children & Youth with Disabilities | Apply EBP. (2019). Retrieved from https://www.applyebp.com/events/train-the-brain-motor-learning-strategies-to-promote-neuroplasticity-in-children-and-youth-with-disabilities/

Treating Insomnia Without Medication. (2019). Retrieved from https://www.brainscienceinstitute.org/brain_talk/treating_insomnia_without_medication

Use It or Lose It: The Principles of Brain Plasticity. (2019). Retrieved from https://articles.mercola.com/sites/articles/archive/2012/12/09/brain-plasticity.aspx

Using Affirmations in the Treatment of Depression – Naturopathic Doctor News and Review. (2019). Retrieved from https://ndnr.com/womens-health/using-affirmations-in-the-treatment-of-depression/

Want to Stay Sharp? Maintain Your Social Brain | UNC Health Talk. (2019). Retrieved from https://healthtalk.unchealthcare.org/want-to-stay-sharp-maintain-your-social-brain/

Washington, J. The Relationship Between Age & Plasticity. (2019). Retrieved from https://sciencing.com/the-relationship-between-age-plasticity-12760666.html

Weiss, D. Do It Yourself EMDR: Is It Possible? Is It Safe?. (2019). Retrieved from https://www.theanxietydocseattle.com/do-it-yourself-emdr-possible-safe/

What are Brainwaves ? Types of Brain waves | EEG sensor and brain wave – UK. (2019). Retrieved from https://brainworksneurotherapy.com/what-are-brainwaves

What Are Glial Cells and What Do They Do?. (2019). Retrieved from https://www.verywellhealth.com/what-are-glial-cells-and-what-do-they-do-4159734

What Causes Learned Helplessness?. (2019). Retrieved from https://www.verywellmind.com/what-is-learned-helplessness-2795326

What is brain plasticity and why is it so important?. (2019). Retrieved from https://theconversation.com/what-is-brain-plasticity-and-why-is-it-so-important-55967

What Is Cognitive Flexibility?. (2019). Retrieved from https://mentalhealthdaily.com/2015/07/24/what-is-cognitive-flexibility/

What is EMDR? | EMDR Institute – EYE MOVEMENT DESENSITIZATION AND REPROCESSING THERAPY. (2019). Retrieved from https://www.emdr.com/what-is-emdr/

What is Neurogenesis and Why is it Important? - Exploring your mind. (2019). Retrieved from https://exploringyourmind.com/what-neurogenesis-why-important/

What is Neuroplasticity?. (2019). Retrieved from https://www.developgoodhabits.com/what-is-neuroplasticity/

What Is Neuroplasticity?. (2019). Retrieved from https://www.brainline.org/author/celeste-campbell/qa/what-neuroplasticity

What is Neuroplasticity? Brain plasticity explained – UK. (2019). Retrieved from https://brainworksneurotherapy.com/what-neuroplasticity

What is procrastination | Procrastination.com. (2019). Retrieved from https://procrastination.com/what-is-procrastination

What Is The "Learned Helplessness" Psychology Definition? | Betterhelp. (2019). Retrieved from https://www.betterhelp.com/advice/behavior/what-is-the-learned-helplessness-psychology-definition/

Bibliography

What Is Trauma? - Definition, Symptoms, Responses, Types & Therapy. (2019). Retrieved from https://integratedlistening.com/what-is-trauma/

Whitney, S. Executive Functioning Skills: Cognitive Flexibility. (2019). Retrieved from http://blog.studentcaffe.com/cognitive-flexibility/

Why a brain-healthy lifestyle is so important. (2019). Retrieved from https://sharpbrains.com/resources/2-the-4-pillars-of-brain-maintenance/why-a-brain-healthy-lifestyle-is-so-important/

Why Change is so Hard: The Chemistry of Habits. (2019). Retrieved from https://medium.com/@MaxWeigand/why-change-is-so-hard-the-chemistry-of-habits-f0c226f00bff

Why Practice Makes Perfect: How to Rewire Your Brain for Performance. (2019). Retrieved from https://buffer.com/resources/why-practice-actually-makes-perfect-how-to-rewire-your-brain-for-better-performance

You Can Trick Your Brain Into Not Procrastinating. (2019). Retrieved from https://motherboard.vice.com/en_us/article/jpg5j3/you-can-trick-your-brain-into-not-procrastinating

www.ingramcontent.com/pod-product-compliance
Lightning Source LLC
Chambersburg PA
CBHW020404080526
44584CB00014B/1162